Into Our Third Century Series

TO PROCLAIM THE FAITH

ALAN K. WALTZ

Alan K. Waltz, Editor

Foreword by
Norman E. Dewire

ABINGDON PRESS   Nashville

TO PROCLAIM THE FAITH

Library of Congress Cataloging in Publication Data

WALTZ, ALAN K.
   To proclaim the faith.
   (Into our third century)
   Includes bibliographical references.
   1. United Methodist Church (U.S.)—Doctrinal and
controversial works. I. Title. II. Series.
BX8382.2.W35   1983   287'.6   83-2700

ISBN 0-687-42252-3

MANUFACTURED BY THE PARTHENON PRESS AT
NASHVILLE, TENNESSEE, UNITED STATES OF AMERICA

To

Mary Joyce

Contents

Acknowledgments

This book is the final volume of seventeen in the Into Our Third Century Series sponsored by the General Council on Ministries. I am deeply grateful to the Council for the time it made available to me for the preparation of this book. The outline for this volume was reviewed in its early stages by two groups related to the Council—the Advisory Group on Research and the Advisory Group on Planning and Futures. Their assistance is deeply appreciated.

A word must be said about the contribution of Ezra Earl Jones to the Into Our Third Century Series. He was the initial project director and the editor of the first eight books. His insights and skills set the tone for the series; he has been of considerable help to me with this book, and throughout the series.

I am especially indebted to Douglas W. Johnson and Robert L. Wilson. They read the manuscript in detail in its various stages of preparation and provided wise counsel and constructive comments.

A special word of appreciation must be expressed to my staff colleagues, Dalila Cruz, Norman E. Dewire, Dee Ann Kahn, C. Leonard Miller, and Royal B. Fishbeck, Jr. In all phases of preparation, they provided counsel as to the direction and content of the book, critiqued the text, and offered support and encouragement.

Special thanks, too, go to Carol Evans Smith for her skilled and patient editorial work, to Mildred Griffiths for her careful and precise proofreading of this and other manuscripts in the series, and to Lola Conrad for her skilled and careful typing of the various drafts, and for her attention to many details throughout much of the series.

And I must also say a word of appreciation and love to Mary Joyce and to our children, Sharon and Reid. They endured with patience and understanding the many hours I have spent in the study, when I should have been with them. Without their love and support, I could not have completed the task.

Alan K. Waltz
April 1983

.

Foreword

"The world is my parish," said John Wesley, describing what it means to be alive with the gospel of Jesus Christ. The Wesleyan vision of holy love and vital piety spread like wildfire across the United States as the frontier expanded. People of all races, cultures, and classes responded to a gospel that proclaimed grace and freedom, offered salvation, and demanded service as the fruit of Christian faith in God. Today the attention of many of us in The United Methodist Church is focused only on our own members. "The world is my parish" has been turned inside out, resulting in "my parish is my world." The wildfire seems to be banked, but it need not stay that way!

The year 1984 marks the 200th anniversary of the formal founding of Methodism in the United States. The United Methodist Church of today is the result of a 1968 merger of the Evangelical United Brethren Church and The Methodist Church, which traces its beginnings to the 1784 Christmas Conference in Baltimore, Maryland. The bicentennial will be a time of great celebration—a time of launching into a third century of proclamation and service by United Methodists. This book, *To Proclaim the Faith*, is offered to you for study, reflection, and action in the name of Jesus the Christ.

In a letter written in 1962, the late Harry Denman, then general secretary of the Methodist Board of Evangelism, stated, "We must help the local congregation to realize that the church must be the church. It is not a club, but the church is Christ living and working in the community." Twenty years later, we face the same challenge! The most important decision facing us in The United Methodist Church of the 1980s will be

11

whether to act as though the world is our parish, or to allow the geographic confines of our parish and our membership list to be the extent of our world! How quickly people busy themselves with church work, while the work of the Church never gets started. In many places the parish has become a club!

Throughout the New Testament, the Church is regarded as an expanding community led by Jesus Christ. Paul's two metaphors of the temple and the body reinforce this idea. Christians are bricks built into the temple, limbs linked together in the Body. While Jesus Christ is the cornerstone of the temple and the head of the Body, there would be no temple without bricks, and no Body without limbs. We are to be more than a pile of bricks or a dismembered corpse! Under the guidance of the Holy Spirit, we are to be a group of believers, caring for one another and reaching out into the community. As United Methodist Christians, we are to be the Church and do the work of the Church. "The world is our parish!"

Paul urged Christians to think of themselves as an organic body. Each part of the body is unique. Each part is seen in the way it reflects, witnesses, and points to the central purpose of the whole. Paul pointed out that Christians are called not as individuals, but as members of a royal priesthood, a holy nation, the temple of the living God, members of the Body of Christ, God's own people. There can be no Body without many members. With different ideas and roles in life, those members acknowledge the common source of their ideas and actions—Jesus Christ. Because they acknowledge this source, the members are bound to one another as members of his Body, living with their differences. Paul wrote about the need for each person to be regarded as part of the Body of Christ. Paul also wrote about what this Body of Christ is to do—what it means to be the Church.

Today, some persons emphasize the nurturing activities of the Church, while others care more for its outreach activities. Some see the primary concern of the Church as the way God enters individual lives, and the primary role of the Church as enabling its members to live in the world as individual Christians who treat social problems. They hope the world will be saved by people joining the Church. Others see the primary concern of the Church as the way God rules in the world, and the primary role of the Church as enabling its members to live in the world as part of a Christian body that prevents social problems. They hope that the world will be saved by people affecting society.

In either case, Paul is quite clear. There are two focuses for the Church. One is the Church itself, and the other is the world in which the Church lives. In the first, Paul is concerned that the Body of Christ be dynamic, have its parts function together, pay attention to itself, feed and sustain its parts, and build on the contribution of all its members. In the second, he is concerned about what the Body is and does. The living parts, working together, are the source of nurture, change, judgment, and direction for the world. As the Body is sent into the world, the people of God are to be a royal priesthood, caring for one another, healing, sacrificing, reconciling, redeeming, and judging.

The nature and duty of the Church are determined by the way Jesus lived and worked. He surrendered himself to the world in the service of God. A church called to be a disciple of Jesus Christ must remember the temptations that stood at the beginning of Jesus' ministry. Led by the Spirit, Jesus entered the desert; led by the same Spirit, the Church enters the world. Jesus accepted this world as the arena; Jesus committed himself to the world. Thus he was able to face the world confidently. He returned from the desert, entering the world as one who had broken the old ways of society and created new ways of living. He was doing the work in the world that God intended for him. Can we accept the world as the arena, the work, that God intends for us? Can we commit ourselves to the world, facing it confidently? Can we do the work that God intends in the world, breaking the old ways of society and creating new ways of living?

All the people of God are called "to walk humbly with the Lord your God." Knowing who we are as a people of God, we are called to bear witness to the ultimate rule of God.

In *The Book of Discipline of The United Methodist Church, 1980,* we read these statements:

A local church is a community of true believers under the Lordship of Christ. . . . The Church exists for the maintenance of worship, the edification of believers, and the redemption of the world" (¶ 201). . . . The Church of Jesus Christ exists in and for the world. It is primarily at the level of the local church that the Church encounters the world. The local church is a strategic base from which Christians move out to the structures of society (¶ 202).

During and after the Protestant Reformation, it was assumed that the local church was a place where people came to hear the Word preached and to have the sacraments duly administered. There was a local church in each village, and it was assumed that the community and society were Christianized. Coming to the church was the task of the individual believer. Around the church building, a "come" structure developed. Frequently, the "come" structure became a "care" station. In many places, a "go" structure also developed. Christian believers *come* to hear the Word and be nurtured; they *go* out with a proclamation of their own. A "go" structure is needed in all local churches! Our motto should always be The World Is My Parish, not My Parish Is My World.

In Proverbs 29:18 (KJV) it is written, "Where there is no vision, the people perish." As United Methodist Christians, we must begin with the mission of Jesus. As his followers, we must be certain of what he came to do and what he expects of us. As Paul said in First Corinthians 14:8 (NEB), "If the trumpet-call is not clear, who will prepare for battle?" When Jesus began his public religious life, he quoted the familiar passage from Isaiah as his own code: "The Spirit of the Lord is upon me. . . . [God has sent me to] preach good news to the poor . . . proclaim release to the captives and recovering of sight to the blind . . . set at liberty those who are oppressed . . . proclaim the acceptable year of the Lord" (Luke 4:18-19 RSV). It is quite clear what Jesus expects of us. God is in charge. Like Jesus, we commit our lives to God. Because we belong to God, we must restore the sense and reality of God's rule in this world.

The Gospel writers give us two clear messages. First is the message of salvation. Through the years, United Methodists have been proclaiming grace and freedom! For Jesus, salvation meant liberation from disease, demons, sin, and exploitation. It meant restoration of physical and mental health, of social and economic relationship, of the whole person in relation to God and to others.

Second, there is the message of service. Jesus did not carry out his mission alone or for his own self-development. He called others to join him. Jesus understood his mission to be based on the concept of the suffering servant in Isaiah. Three chapters of The Gospel According to Mark make it clear that Jesus intended for his disciples to give their lives in service:

—If you would come after me, first deny yourself and take up your cross and follow me (8:34).
—You who would save your life will lose it, and you who lose your life will save it (8:35).
—What does it profit you to gain the whole world and forfeit your life? (8:36).
—If you would be first, you must be last of all and servant of all (9:35).
—Those who do not receive the kingdom of God as a child shall not enter it (10:15).
—How hard it will be for those who have riches to enter the kingdom of God (10:23).
—Many that are first will be last, and the last first (10:31).
—Those who would be great among you must be servants of all (10:44).

Hence followers of Jesus the Christ are expected to make a total commitment of self-giving service.

Just as salvation and service are the two major themes for faithful followers of Jesus Christ, so they are the two major tenets of life within The United Methodist Church. Those who join The United Methodist Church are asked to respond positively to the following question: "Will you be loyal to The United Methodist Church and uphold it by your prayers, your presence, your gifts, and your service?" The prayers we pledge are the fruit of our lips, as the gifts we pledge are the fruit of our labors. We pledge our presence at congregational gatherings for study, celebration, worship as an act of witness within the community, and the planning or promoting of some

part of the total mission of the church. The service we pledge
includes our participation in the life of the congregation as well
as our expansion into the community and the larger world with
the power of the love of God as experienced in Jesus Christ.

As United Methodist Christians, we are more than a pile of
bricks or a dismembered corpse! We are the temple of the
living God. We are the Body of Christ *and* what the Body of
Christ is expected to do. Our United Methodist local churches
exist primarily as strategic bases from which we encounter the
world. Does our local church have only a "come" structure, or
does it have a "go" structure as well? Is the world our parish, or
have we let our parish become our world?

Our founders emphasized evangelism, the spreading of
scriptural holiness throughout the land, both by proclaiming
grace and freedom and by seeking justice and peace. The
bicentennial of The United Methodist Church is a time for us to
pause and reflect on the way the Wesleyan vision of holy love
and vital piety *has* spread throughout the United States of
America. In 1977 the Council of Bishops and the General
Council on Ministries jointly created the Bicentennial Planning
Committee to recommend ways for United Methodists to
observe the 200th anniversary of the founding of Methodism
in the United States. The committee's report was adopted by
the 1980 General Conference. Referring to the formal
beginning of the Methodist movement in the United States at
the 1784 Christmas Conference, the committee stated, "From
this Conference, American Methodism expanded under God's
grace to eventually touch the vital fabric of an emerging
people. [We] began as a minority movement which expanded
to become a major influence in American culture. . . . We have
been both committed and selfish, both redemptive and
repressive. For the times we have been Christlike, we thank
God for empowerment. For the times we have failed, we are
given courage by God's forgiveness."

The bicentennial is also a time to reflect on what United
Methodists are *doing* in communities across this land and
throughout the world. The Bicentennial Planning Committee
stated further, "To avoid the possibility of both excessive
nostalgia and unrealistic futurism, a primary focus of the

Bicentennial will be the present." This book, *To Proclaim the Faith*, is one way United Methodists can reflect on the present time.

The bicentennial further provides a time to *launch* The United Methodist Church into a third century of witness and service. The committee continued,

> As we approach the end of our second century, we look forward with excitement and hope to the beginning of a third century in the service of our Lord. Our concern is that, through our recognition of the past and our affirmation of the present, we will be called into the future as new beings, refreshed by our experience of Christ, revived in our commitments to bring salvation, peace, and justice to all of God's children, and renewed as a people of God in our own time. . . . Building on what we have learned from the past and experienced in the present, we will boldly launch the third century of United Methodism empowered by the Holy Spirit, obedient to the Christ, and thankful for the constant grace of our Creator.

We have a rich heritage. As the young nation grew, our forebears influenced the shape of the nation's ideals and realities. As needs arose, churches, schools, hospitals, homes, and other action ministries developed. Our growth and influence are impressive and should be celebrated along with our errors, neglects, and need for repentance. As the Bicentennial Planning Committee reported to the 1980 General Conference,

> An energetic and stubborn people, we have been guilty at times of moving away from the direction of the Spirit. However, our internal diversity, our balance between the pursuit of personal holiness and social justice, and our ongoing commitment to the call to Christ have again and again brought us back to the doing of our Maker's will. Both our joys and our sorrows, our victories and our defeats need to be claimed, celebrated, and lifted up for the world to see.

The present, as the time in which we live, is between the past and the future. Let us celebrate the present, as well as claim the past. In the committee's words, the present. . .

is a representation of what we are, what we have been or might
have been, and what we can become through the grace of God.
Both our experience of the past and our expectations of the
future are reflected in our present action. . . . This is true as
we minister to human need, proclaim the love of God, heal the
sick, feed the hungry, defend the poor, proclaim grace and
freedom, preach the Word, and serve as agents of God for
reconciliation in the world of today.

But it is not enough merely to claim the past and celebrate the
present. Jesus Christ calls us to be his Body. Life is a constantly
moving and changing reality. We live in the present, influenced
by the past, but we work for the City of God as it will be in the
future. We must challenge the future, for it will be influenced
by the way we think, act, and feel today. It is not beyond our
own making. We must project the future we want, and then
work for that future. We can determine the new day in United
Methodism! We can boldly move into our third century with
the power of the Holy Spirit, being obedient to Jesus Christ and
grateful for the grace of our Creator God.

As United Methodists, you and I are invited to reflect on our
church's meaning for the future. Each of us must experience
anew the sense of mission and purpose that filled our
predecessors with the power to proclaim grace and freedom
and to work for justice and peace. Can we again commit
sufficient spiritual and material resources for evangelism and
social justice to make a difference in the volatile, struggling,
secular world of the late 1900s? Can we keep organizational
problems and internal differences from diverting the energy
needed to pursue the goals of the gospel? Can we affirm who
we are as United Methodists? Can we assess what is happening
in our world, our nation, our parishes? Can we assess what
other people of faith are doing, and what new avenues of
ministry are available to enable us to be the people of God who
make a difference in the world of today and tomorrow?

These and other questions led the General Council on
Ministries, with encouragement from the Council of Bishops,
to engage in a Research Design for United Methodism as It
Enters Its Third Century. This seven-year project has been
intended to aid the entire denomination to engage in

discussion about who we are as United Methodists, what we wish to accomplish, and how we pursue our goals in the years ahead. The total series of seventeen books, listed opposite the title page of this book, has now been published through Abingdon Press. Each has been based on an individually commissioned study or research project. These books are intended to open discussion in local churches, districts, annual conference groups, and general agencies about issues of critical concern in the life of The United Methodist Church.

Although each of these studies was done separately, the various authors seem to mention four major themes more frequently than any others:

1. The United Methodist Church must rediscover much of its Wesleyan tradition. It must rekindle the sense of spiritual urgency and commitment to Christ that characterized the early Methodist societies.

2. The United Methodist Church must empower and motivate the laity for proclamation and service. Our denomination must avoid being an institution controlled by a profession-oriented clergy and become a denomination in which the laity are strengthened in their commitment to carry the gospel into the world.

3. The United Methodist Church must restate its sense of common identity and purpose. By so doing, it will be better able to witness with power and clarity and make a difference in the quality of people's lives.

4. The United Methodist Church must focus on its evangelistic outreach. It must turn its primary attention and energies to evangelization of the world, nurture of Christian believers, and service and advocacy for persons in need.

It is our responsibility as United Methodists to rediscover our roots in the Wesleyan tradition, and then to develop creative plans that can be discussed, agreed upon, and lived out. What has made The United Methodist Church significant? What can make it significant tomorrow?

To Proclaim the Faith addresses these questions. Alan Waltz has drawn on insights gained from the Into Our Third Century Series. He summarizes our history, describes how faith was put into action, examines the meaning of vital piety, shows what it means to be the local church, challenges us to rediscover scriptural holiness, displays ways in which United Methodism has been at work for justice and peace, and then focuses on the potential for our third century. We are to proclaim the faith, build the Church, and serve the world!

We commend *To Proclaim the Faith* to you for study and as a springboard toward action in local church classes, organizations, and discussion groups. The book has been written so that it can be used in a variety of ways, including as curriculum for a church school "quarter." Study questions are found at the end of each chapter. As reflections and action plans result from your reading and study of this book, we invite you to share them with others in your local church and to discuss ideas and plans with district, conference, and general church leaders. Your responses will be welcomed by the members and staff of the General Council on Ministries.

United Methodists are believers in the resurrection of Jesus the Christ. This is the basis of our assurance and hope. We are called to make a difference in this world. We are a resurrection people. We are also a people of the Pentecost, knowing that the power of the Holy Spirit abides in each of us. We hold the power to mold the future. Joining with the words of the Bicentennial Planning Committee's report to the 1980 General Conference, it is our prayer that that occasion "will be a call to a new birth of the fervent spirit of Methodism, to a new birth of personal obedience to the Christ, to a new birth of creative local congregations, to a new birth of evangelical zeal, and to a new birth of our vital commitment to peace and social justice."

Norman E. Dewire
General Secretary
General Council on Ministries
601 West Riverview Avenue
Dayton, Ohio 45406

April 1983

CHAPTER 1

A People of the Assurance

"It was the best of times, it was the worst of times, it was the age of wisdom, it was the age of foolishness, it was the epoch of belief, it was the epoch of incredulity, it was the season of Light, it was the season of Darkness, it was the spring of hope, it was the winter of despair." Such were the times of which Charles Dickens wrote, and such were the times in which John Wesley lived—times of extraordinary contrasts and enormous transitions.

During the Industrial Revolution, the agricultural age was giving way to an economy and society based on factory production. Great wealth began to shift from the landed aristocracy to city merchants and factory owners, evidenced by the grand houses in the rapidly growing cities and surrounding towns. In sharp contrast were the overcrowded, more modest areas and poverty-filled slums which housed the unskilled and semiskilled who, forced off the land, had migrated to the cities in search of jobs. There human misery abounded. All in England were striving to adjust to these profound changes, to find their places in the new social and economic order, to search for ways to sustain themselves, to find meaning in the midst of shifting values. Such were the conditions during Wesley's time.

Today, we too live in a period of significant transition. Our present shift away from the Industrial Revolution and into the Information Revolution is the Third Wave, or the Post-Industrial Age, of which Alvin Toffler, Daniel Bell, and many others are writing. Industry and production are yielding to the processing and exchange of information as the economic basis of our society. Once again, the sources of power and wealth are shifting. No longer held solely by the owners and managers of great industrial organizations, wealth and power are now falling into the hands of those who possess and process information. Simultaneously and inevitably, the unskilled and semiskilled are being released from their industrial-based jobs. Because occupations no longer match or are beyond their skills, these people languish in unemployment. The population is migrating away from the cities to those parts of the country that can provide jobs. Again people are seeking to adjust to profound changes, to find their places in the new social and economic order, to discover ways to sustain themselves, and to find meaning in the midst of shifting values. Such is the time in which we as United Methodists live and work.

After the current transition, what will be the nature of our society? What will it mean for us—individually, as Christians, and collectively, as United Methodists? As United Methodists today, we are tentative and uncertain about our message and direction. While we are engaged in many tasks, frequently we are not certain of our reasons or goals. We seek guidance for this time of transition, help in focusing on decisions we must make, and motivation for channeling our lives and resources toward the worship and service of God.

What encouraged and uplifted those who preceded us in the faith? *Our forebears found their purpose as a people of God in simple yet profound tasks: Proclaim the faith, build the Church, serve the world.* Our denomination traces its beginnings in this country back to 1784. When the United States received its formal independence, John Wesley felt it was time for his followers in the new nation to become an autonomous church. With his guidance, the new denomination was born at the Christmas Conference held in Baltimore in 1784. It began during a time of change for the society and the nation. It has grown in times of stress. Now we must reflect on our task in a nation and a world that are undergoing new tensions and strains.

Our challenge is to find the resolve and assurance to move into and through our third century with power and conviction. Perhaps our earlier purposes merely need to be restated with clarity, affirmed with conviction, and realized with dedication. Let it be our goal that United Methodists will look back in 2084 and rejoice in the renewed vitality and commitment developed and sustained during our third century.

So let us join together to search for that new spirit of conviction and resolve. The present "is the best of times and the worst of times." The future can be either. You and I—as United Methodists, as a people of God—will have a major role in determining whether the times will be the best or the worst—both in the present and in the future.

This book has a special purpose. It is to reflect on the distance United Methodists have traveled in the United States. It is to understand our unique character as a people of God, both today and in the future. But most important, it is to challenge you, both as an individual and as a United Methodist, to explore your commitment: Proclaim the faith, build the Church, serve the world. Let us once again bring into sharp focus our purpose and resolve; let us again proclaim with power the words of Charles Wesley's hymn!

> A charge to keep I have,
> A God to glorify,
> A never-dying soul to save,
> And fit it for the sky.
>
> To serve the present age,
> My calling to fulfill;
> O may it all my powers engage
> To do my Master's will!

Hearts Strangely Warmed

John Wesley: A Conversion and a Movement Begun

As United Methodists, we trace our heritage to John Wesley (1703–1791). He lived in an uneasy time in his native England. Many people were oppressed, downtrodden, cut off from the church. Others with education and some measure of wealth lacked an active concern about both their Christian faith and the problems of poor and working-class people.

Wesley was a lifelong member of the Church of England. His father, Samuel Wesley, served as pastor for thirty-nine years in the small village of Epworth in the English midlands, and there John Wesley grew up. Although his family had little money, John did receive a good education and was graduated from

Oxford University. Ordained a priest in the Church of England, he remained so until his death.

Throughout his early adult life, however, Wesley searched for a motivating power. A brief period as a missionary in Georgia was of no help, and while his travels in Europe and study among the early Moravians and German United Brethren (Unitas Fretas) provided insights, he did not find the unifying concepts for his life there.

It was at a meeting on Aldersgate Street on May 24, 1738, that John Wesley found his spiritual rebirth—that inner witness he had so long sought. He recorded the event in his Journal: "About a quarter before nine . . . I felt my heart strangely warmed. I felt I did trust in Christ, Christ alone for salvation; and an assurance was given me that He had taken away *my* sins, even *mine,* and saved *me* from the law of sin and death."[1]

Thus Wesley sensed that he was restored in love to God. With this experience came a sense of vocation that was to be the mainstay of his life and work. In 1756 he wrote that his one purpose in life was "to promote, so far as I am able, vital, practical religion; and by the grace of God to beget, preserve, and increase the life of God in the souls of men."[2]

And promote practical religion, increase the life of God in the souls of people, he did. In Wesley's preaching and writing two key concepts were emphasized. First was the *sense of assurance* that God had acted on behalf of each of us. Christ came that we might be forgiven of our sins through faith and repentance. Because we are forgiven, we are now fully and completely restored in love to God. Forgiveness and reconciliation are available to each of us, Wesley assured the people of his day, and of ours as well. We must but believe in Christ, receive the blessing of the grace of God, and live in thankfulness and service to God. The concept was not new, but Wesley gave it a new dynamic power by stressing that it is available to each person who believes in Christ. It was an assurance that God's grace can be received and is to be shared. "Never before in the history of the Church since the writings of St. Paul had the doctrines of Assurance been so clearly enunciated."[3]

Wesley's second emphasis was the *concept of Christian*

perfection. He taught that it is possible to move toward full and complete perfection in God, both in this life and the next. Like the assurance of forgiveness of sins, this is a gracious gift from God. Each of us can come into a more complete relationship with God through Christ. This doctrine, which produced considerable misunderstanding in Wesley's lifetime, is still not well understood. Wesley was convinced that it is indeed possible to move on in this life toward greater vitality in our Christian faith and into a more perfect relationship with God.

Albert Outler put it this way: "Wesley . . . was adamant on the point that if 'perfection' is a human possibility at all, it must at least be possible *in the span of human life* and, consequently, correlated with the whole process of Christian maturation and hope. . . . For Wesley, the doctrine of perfection was yet another way of celebrating the *sovereignty* of grace!"[4]

Wesley's concept of holiness embraced these two concepts. Holiness reflects (1) full assurance of the achievement of one's faith, and (2) both the absence of moral impurities and imperfection in one's life and the presence of the purity of love. Wesley believed that through God's grace, it is possible for each person to achieve this state of holiness, even in this life. The Christian's goal, as Wesley saw it, is to move toward this holiness, this perfection.

For Wesley and the early Methodists, commitment to the future rested on the twin emphases of assurance and perfection—both for the individual and for society. How could one believe in God's gift of grace freely given to each person—along with the possibility of moving toward Christian perfection—and not be stirred to action? Wesley's emphasis on assurance and perfection gave his early followers their power for preaching and proclaiming the faith. Theirs was a commitment to the future—in this world and the next.

This was a commitment to the individual's salvation, made possible through Christ—a salvation available to all, to be received and responded to in faith. Yet it was also a commitment to society. If it is possible for all persons to move on toward perfection of the Christian life in this world, then the same must be possible for society as a whole. The Christian, then, must use available resources to improve the settings in which all persons live out their lives in response to God's creative activity.

The people of assurance—as Methodists and their United Brethren and Evangelical counterparts were often characterized —were the people of hope and of the future. They saw the possibilities of the new land, the potential of the individual— always in the context of what God in Christ had done and could do in their lives and in their society. This sense of assurance and of the future gave early Americans in the United Methodist tradition the strength to respond to the challenge of the frontier, where circuit riders went wherever necessary to proclaim the faith to individuals. The commitment made it possible to marshal the resources necessary to establish congregations, to build the church, and to create the great ministries of outreach. The sense of assurance provided the power to respond to and serve the world through the major missionary movements of the nineteenth and twentieth centuries.

Our Beginnings in England and in the United States

John Wesley's work took two forms which continued throughout his life. First, he resolved to tell as many people as possible of his convictions about the assurance of God's forgiveness and redemption. He wanted all who would listen to know that it was possible to find a new relationship with God in this life and in the next. He visited prisons and, following the lead of George Whitfield, began to "preach in the fields." At first Wesley was not comfortable with this approach, but he soon realized that in this way he could reach many who would not or could not come to the churches. (Subsequently, Wesley was often denied the opportunity of preaching in many of the established [Church of England] churches, including the one his own father had served.)

Second, Wesley understood that new converts needed to be aided in their growth and encouraged in their faith. He had seen how some of the "societies" of the German United Brethren and the Moravians guided and strengthened persons in their faith; he knew that small groups could nurture the faith of their Christian participants. Because few clergy were available to help those who responded to Wesleyan preaching, it was essential that members of these groups or "societies" care for and support one another in their spiritual journeys. Wesley encouraged the development of these societies, which were essentially developed under lay leadership.

Wesley preached intensively for two years following his Aldersgate experience and helped to establish a few societies, particularly in Bristol. Although he was still participating in a Moravian society in London, it became increasingly clear that he could not agree with some of their theological principles, and on July 23, 1740, he formed his own society in the Foundry, an old building he had recently purchased. With the beginning of this United Society, composed of forty-eight women and twenty-five men, the Methodist movement started its organizational journey. Proclaiming the faith and building the church through societies, it gathered strength and spread throughout England with surprising rapidity. It soon became apparent that the time had come for the movement to consider how best to serve the world.

How did Methodism get its start in the United States? It began rather informally. Followers of Wesley emigrated to America, and societies were formed and led by unofficial lay preachers. It is not possible to document the first. The following statement appeared in the 1787 and in several succeeding editions of *The Discipline,* and describes the early development of the Methodist movement.

> During the space of thirty years past, certain persons, members of the society, emigrated from England and Ireland, and settled in various parts of this country. About twenty years ago, Philip Embury, a local preacher from Ireland, began to preach in the city of New York, and formed a society of his own countrymen and the citizens. About the same time, Robert Strawbridge, a local preacher from Ireland, settled in Frederic county in the state of Maryland, and preaching there, formed some societies. In 1769, Richard Boardman and Joseph Pilmoor, came to New-York; who were the first regular Methodist Preachers on the continent.[5]

So it was that the "planting of Methodism" in this country was accomplished by lay people. The early Methodist societies in and around Baltimore, Philadelphia, and New York began to flourish, purchasing or constructing their own buildings. Philip Embury, Barbara Heck, Betty (a slave), Thomas Webb, and Thomas Taylor, members of the John Street Society in New York, were concerned about the orderly and continuing growth of the Methodist movement. The first Wesleyan preachers were sent to this country in response to a letter from Thomas Taylor and the New York group. Part of that earnest appeal of 1767 reads: "We must have a man of wisdom, of sound faith, and a good disciplinarian—one whose heart and soul are in the work; and I doubt not but, by the goodness of God, such a flame would be kindled as would never stop, until it reached the great South Sea. . . . Dear Sir, I entreat you, for the good of thousands, to use your utmost endeavors to send one over."[6]

The Methodist conference in England gave careful consideration to the request, and between 1769 and 1774, twelve preachers came to America, either under Wesley's direct appointment or with only his consent. Among the first to arrive were Joseph Pilmoor and Richard Boardman, who worked primarily in the New York and Philadelphia areas. Francis Asbury, who arrived in 1771 and possessed a special understanding of the temperament of the emerging nation, was well received and remained in this country. All those early preachers worked under the direct guidance and scrutiny of John Wesley.

As the work of Methodism prospered, the beginnings of organization were established. Thomas Rankin and Francis Asbury were appointed as Wesley's general assistants, and the first conference of American Methodism was held in July, 1773, with ten clergymen in attendance.

The movement was gaining strong headway by the time the American Revolution began. The war was a devastating blow to American Methodists because of their close ties with Wesley and England. Many of the clergy returned to England, and there arose a concern about providing the sacraments. Wesley would not allow unordained preachers to administer the sacraments, and he tried in vain to have some of his preachers ordained by American bishops of the Church of England. With the increasing number of societies, he realized the need for Methodists to be able to participate in the sacraments.

The United States acquired full political independence on September 3, 1783, when England and the United States signed the Treaty of Paris. At this point Wesley began to consider making the Methodist movement in the United States independent of his immediate and personal direction, and he concluded that he must ordain pastors to be sent to direct the work. "On September 2, 1784, in Bristol, England, John Wesley performed the ordinations that were to make possible the establishment of an independent Methodist Church in the newly created nation."[7] Richard Whatcoat and Thomas Vasey were ordained as ministers that day, and Thomas Coke, a minister of the Church of England, was designated a general superintendent of the new church.

The group arrived with specific instructions for the new church and for the appointment of Thomas Coke and Francis Asbury as general superintendents. So it was that some sixty persons gathered at Lovely Lane Chapel in Baltimore, Maryland, in late December 1784 to establish The Methodist Episcopal Church. Thus the people of the assurance formally began their journey in the United States.

While the Methodist movement is firmly rooted in English backgrounds and culture, the Evangelical and United Brethren movements trace their histories to German peoples and traditions.

Philip William Otterbein (1726–1813) was instrumental in the development of the United Brethren movement in the United States. Born and educated in Germany, Otterbein was an ordained minister of the German Reformed Church. He came as a missionary to this country in 1752 and served several parishes. In 1774, partly at the urging of Francis Asbury, he became pastor of a German Reformed congregation in Baltimore and held that post for the remainder of his life.

A close associate of Otterbein was Martin Boehm. Together they led a revival movement during the late 1700s among the German populations of Pennsylvania, Maryland, and Virginia. In 1800, several German pastors met to consider what they might be able to accomplish in cooperation. Otterbein and

Boehm were selected as superintendents, or bishops, of the new group. It was not until their General Conference of 1815, however, that the Church of the United Brethren in Christ took on definite organizational form and content. The new denomination was established along lines followed by the Methodists, with most of the material from the Methodist *Discipline* being used as a foundation for its organization and work.

"The Evangelical Association originated mostly in the same areas of Pennsylvania, Maryland, and Virginia as the United Brethren, but several decades later."[8] Jacob Albright (1759–1808) is considered the founder of the Evangelical Association movement. Raised in a German-speaking family in the United States, he was essentially self-taught. He spent his early adult years as a farmer, and in 1791, "under the influence of a Reformed minister, a Methodist local preacher, and a lay preacher with the Otterbein Movement, he was converted and joined a Methodist class meeting which was nearby. He was strongly attracted to the spiritual atmosphere of this class meeting and was also favorably impressed by the Methodist organization."[9]

Soon Albright began to preach and organize societies. While his early work was highly localized, it eventually spread through much of eastern Pennsylvania. Albright died before his movement was fully organized, but his work was carried on by George Miller, who prepared the first *Discipline* of the movement, patterned after that of the Methodists. The first General Conference of Albright's People met in 1816 in Union County, Pennsylvania, and took the name Evangelical Association.

Thus the three groups were established. In the early years, the interconnections among them were many: Otterbein participated in the consecration of Asbury at the Christmas Conference of 1784; Asbury may have been influential in Otterbein's accepting the call to the congregation in Baltimore; Albright was influenced by Methodist and United Brethren preachers and societies. Throughout the years that followed, the three groups had continuing contacts and conversations, since they were similar in doctrine, social concern, and form of church government.

In the course of their histories, all three groups had several internal divisions and reunions. The slavery issue caused the first major division among Methodists, and differences in interpretation of church administration and doctrine caused other groups to break away. Yet the fundamental core of polity and theology overcame social and other matters that had caused division, and in 1939, three major streams of Methodism, the Methodist Episcopal Church, the Methodist Episcopal Church, South, and the Methodist Protestant Church united to form The Methodist Church. In 1946, the Church of the United Brethren in Christ joined the Evangelical Church to create the Evangelical United Brethren Church. Most recently, after extended conversations, the Evangelical United Brethren Church and The Methodist Church merged in 1968 to form The United Methodist Church.

That union brought together common heritages and concerns. The organizational beginnings can be traced back to that significant Christmas Conference of 1784 when the Methodist movement was established in this nation—independent of, and yet in vital connection with John Wesley. The concepts of assurance, of going on to perfection in God's love, of a vital piety and renewal, drew these people together under a common banner. Now as members in a single denomination, we can rejoice in the richness of our heritage and continue to proclaim the faith, build the Church, and serve the world!

A People Called United Methodist

Our Unique Character—A People Under Conviction

Who are we then, this people called United Methodist? What distinguishes our church from other patterns of life and thought that came out of the Protestant Reformation? What is it that makes us unique?

1. We are a people who believe firmly in the assurance of God's action in and for our lives. Wesley emphasized that through faith in Christ, we can receive God's forgiveness.

Further, there is the possibility that we can move toward the perfection of love in the restored relationship with God. "In *The Message of the Wesleys* Philip Watson has summarized the Wesleyan message as follows: 'All men need to be saved; all men can be saved; all men can know they are saved; all men can be saved to the uttermost.' That is what Wesley had in mind when he discussed 'our doctrines,' that is, those theological emphases which have a special place in the Methodist understanding of Christian faith."[10]

What does this mean for us? It means that United Methodism has been powered by the belief that salvation is available to all who hear its message. Wesley was convinced that all people can come into that restored relationship with God through repentance. It does not require a specific ritual performed in an exact manner. It does not require a precise formulation of words. What it does require is the placing of oneself fully and unreservedly into the hands of God through repentance. When this is done in faith, there is assurance of reconciliation, through grace provided in Jesus Christ.

In part, this is what John Wesley was telling us in his great sermon "The Scripture Way of Salvation," first published in 1765.

> If you seek it [salvation] by faith, you may expect it *as you are*; and if as you are, then expect it *now*. It is of importance to observe, that there is an inseparable connexion between these three points—expect it *by faith;* expect it *as you are;* and expect it *now*. To deny one of them, is to deny them all; to allow one, is to allow them all. Do *you* believe we are sanctified by faith? Be true then to your principle; and look for this blessing just as you are, neither better nor worse; as a poor sinner that has still nothing to pay, nothing to plead, but "Christ *died*." And if you look for it as you are, then expect it *now*. Stay for nothing: why should you? Christ is ready; and He is all you want. He is waiting for you: He is at the door![11]

2. We are a people who believe that we can perfect our relationship with God. Wesley believed it possible for all of us to grow more completely in the love of God in our lives. We can grow and develop—perfect, if you will—our relationship with

God, beginning now. This is possible not only for us as we respond in faith to Christ, but for all people, if they but hear and receive the message of Christ. We believe that *everyone* can know the healing and restoring power of God and that *everyone* has the potential to move into a perfected relationship with God in this life and the next. Therefore, we can improve our own lives and the lives of others.

3. We are a people who believe that we must proclaim the faith, build the Church, and serve the world. Our forebears in the faith realized that if they believed that each person could receive the full assurance of forgiveness of sins now and had the potential to move into perfection in love with God, they must act. One cannot hold that conviction and fail to act.

We are a people who firmly believe that we must witness to God's love and forgiveness. This has been a driving force behind United Methodism throughout its history. If we are truly convinced that the assurance of God's forgiveness is available to all, then we must act, so that all people can hear this good news. The power of this conviction has given rise to the preaching outreach of the denomination, to the nurturing of believers, and to the serving of people regardless of their location or station in life. This surety of faith in Christ, coupled with the belief that we can move to a more complete relationship with God, has provided the dynamic power that has resulted in the movement we call United Methodism.

4. We are a people who believe that our faith is to be experienced, not debated. Our theology is to become a vital part of our daily lives and to provide the motivating power in our relationships with God and with others. This is our first concern. We do not place primary importance on a stated creed or on a prescribed confession to which all must adhere.[12]

Frequently in the course of his career, John Wesley was placed in the position of having to defend the nature of his movement. It was attacked as being both "too religious" and "not religious enough." His statement titled "The Character of a Methodist," in which he tried to explain what he and his followers believed, warrants reading and study in its entirety. First he outlined those traits that do not distinguish us from others, next he described those traits that would identify a

Methodist, and then he summed up: "These are the true marks of a true Methodist. . . . If any man say, 'Why, these are only the common, fundamental principles of Christianity!' Thou hast said: so I mean; this is the very truth. I know they are no other . . . [but] the common principles of Christianity—the plain old Christianity that I teach."[13] He closed with these words:

> By these marks, by these fruits of a living faith, do we labor to distinguish ourselves from the unbelieving world, from all those whose minds or lives are not according to the Gospel of Christ. But from early Christians, of whatsoever denomination they be, we earnestly desire not to be distinguished at all; not from any who sincerely follow after what they know they have not yet attained. . . . And I beseech you, brethren, by the mercies of God, that we be in no wise divided among ourselves. Is thy heart right, as my heart is with thine? I ask no further question: If it be, give me thy hand. For opinions or terms let us not destroy the work of God. Dost thou love and serve God? It is enough. I give thee the right hand of fellowship. If there be any consolation in Christ, if any comfort of love, if any fellowship of the Spirit . . . let us strive together for the faith of the Gospel, walking worthy of the vocation wherewith we are called; with all lowliness and meekness, with long suffering, forebearing one another in love, endeavoring to keep the unity of the Spirit in the bonds of peace, remembering there is one body and one Spirit, even as we are called with one hope of our calling, "one Lord, one faith, one baptism, one God and Father of all, who is above all, and through all, and in you all."[14]

5. We are a people who share two hundred years of history in this nation. And we are a people who share two great Protestant streams of service. The historical statement that was a part of the 1968 uniting document for The Methodist Church and The Evangelical United Brethren Church put it this way:

> Since their beginnings they had lived and worked side by side in friendly fellowship. Had it not been for the difference in language—the Methodist working among English-speaking people and the Evangelical and United Brethren working

among those speaking German—they might, from the beginning, have been one church. Today the language barrier is gone and the uniting of forces for our common task and calling seems appropriate and timely.[15]

We are joined together as United Methodists, recalling a heritage of great proclamation and service. We are humbled, as well, as we remember the divisions, tensions, injustices, and problems that have beset our denomination through the years. Both our successes and our failures have contributed to our present unique character. May this heritage be the basis for discovering our purpose for the future.

The Importance of Our Character Today and Tomorrow

Wesley, Otterbein, and Albright sought to revitalize the individual in relation to God—to indicate anew that each person can come into that saving relationship. Our founders emphasized assurance that this is not only possible, but readily available to all who are sincerely willing to repent and reorder their lives. Through those reordered lives the impact of the Christian faith was to be seen most fully in service and witness to the total society.

How do we see ourselves today in relation to our beginnings and our two-hundred year heritage? How do we see our future?

1. We, as United Methodists, are a people of the assurance of God. Wesley taught that each of us by faith can come into a new relationship with God. Today we must embrace anew the assurance that God's grace is available to us through our sincere willingness to receive it. We must accept anew the possibility of our moving toward perfection in love in relationship with God.

Together, the twin concepts of assurance and perfection are an enormously powerful motivating force. They give us reason to converse with people about their relationships with God. Here is the dynamic power behind preaching and witnessing. This message speaks directly to the needs of the individual. And it is a message which, once received, cannot be contained. It must be shared!

Our founders were not concerned with either the form of the

message or the organization that supported it. Their concern was with the individual's relationship to God and all that it implied as the individual sought to live out this new relationship in the world.

> The concerns of the formative figures in United Methodist theology were focused on the work of God in transforming lives and communities. Albright and Otterbein thought it more fitting to concentrate on conversion of men and women, than on abstract theological speculation. Before them, John Wesley was urged by his mother, Susannah, to subordinate speculation to the practical venture of healing souls.[16]

2. We, as United Methodists, must proclaim the faith. The driving force behind our early heritage was the proclamation of the faith for the salvation of the individual. But commitment to witness and service accompanied the individual's new relationship with God, and that commitment produced United Methodism's great concern for preaching and improving the situation of all people.

The proclamation of the faith was followed by the building of the Church—the nurturing of those who came into the Christian fellowship. Since the earliest societies, followers of the United Methodist tradition have been urged to participate actively and collectively in the worship of God, the encouragement of one another's growth in Christian discipleship, and the collective support of the Christian endeavor. This support has not been limited to the local congregation, but has included the whole Body of Christ. Through participation in the building of the Church Universal, United Methodists reach beyond themselves to assist others, to proclaim the faith in Christ's name throughout the world.

The call to be in fellowship with God requires that we share the faith, nurture those who respond, and serve those in need. United Methodists must explore ways these responsibilities can be met in the future. We must respond creatively and effectively.

3. We, as United Methodists, must not lose sight of the individual. In the complexities of modern society we often

focus our concerns on major systems and issues. As a large denomination, we frequently find our attention drawn to organizational and structural issues. Yet we must take great care that the concerns and needs of the individual are not lost or subordinated while we discuss programs, budgets, and complex social problems.

We experienced denominational growth when we focused on the individual in need of God's grace and on every person's potential for growth in love. This emphasis on the individual must permeate the character of our denomination in the years ahead, if we are to maintain our relevance. The call remains the same—witness to God's love, to each individual, in whatever we do. The extent to which we are willing and able to answer this call will have great impact on our future course and character as a denomination.

4. We, as United Methodists, must witness to the possibility of redemption. We must use the great power that resides in the witness of one individual to another.

At first glance, our forebears seem to have had little strength. But because they were committed to their task and willing to witness to their faith, they were able to accomplish far more than they envisioned.

Today our denomination has great resources. In addition to financial and organizational resources, we have available the enormous power of our individual and collective witness to what God has done in our lives. Although we United Methodists are a dedicated and well-meaning people, in recent years we have become preoccupied with our own institutional and personal concerns. We count our strengths in the wrong terms. We have focused on those things which preserve our lives, rather than on proclamation of our faith and service to others.

In our early years, we did not take the great resources of a large organization to the people—we took the message of God, as reflected in our own deep personal commitment and concern. Then we used the organizations that were available to assist and affirm those persons. When we begin to rely again on the great power that is born of conviction and made known in witness and proclamation, our strength will be renewed.

5. We, as United Methodists, must determine and reaffirm our central purpose, which is clearly defined by our heritage. Our predecessors' organization and structure were directed to a highly specific task, and we must once again make that task clear. It may be a contemporary restatement of the early challenges of Wesley, Albright, and Otterbein. It may be a ringing call for witness and service uniquely responsive to present times. Whatever it is, we must develop a clear consensus for harnessing the denomination's enormous potential for the years ahead.

6. We, as United Methodists, must affirm our collective efforts to accomplish our tasks in God's name. From the beginning, we organized ourselves to accomplish major goals "in connection" with one another. Our development in this country was not as an association of congregations, but as a people committed to accomplishing outreach and mission. Indeed, our first organizational structures—conferences—were designed to deploy and underwrite preachers. That was their primary focus, not the developing and strengthening of the conference or even of the local societies. There was a common conviction that such a great task needed the combined efforts of all those "in connection" with one another.

The efforts of those in the United Methodist heritage have produced one of the largest Protestant denominations in the United States. United Methodist churches are found in every state and in almost every county. We have established colleges, universities, hospitals, facilities for the aged, institutions for children and youth, and many other service organizations all across the land. Many community service agencies are directly owned and operated, or at least partially underwritten by the denomination. We have sent missionaries throughout the world and have taken under our umbrella of concern an extraordinary array of organizations, institutions, issues, and concerns.

Conditions have changed for the denomination. Today United Methodists as a whole do not manifest the driving force to proclaim and witness that characterized our forebears. Today each group within the denomination tends to view its own immediate needs as primary. Local congregations are inclined to address their own needs before turning to the needs of others. Ministers and officials often let their own professional concerns take priority over their primary task. Agencies, institutions, and interest groups of the denomination struggle and preserve themselves, *their* resources, *their* prerogatives. Narrow perspectives have replaced the broader goals of the denomination as a whole. Because the denomination has been unable to present a clear and cogent statement of its major tasks and roles, there has been a loss of commitment to the overall life of the church.

As a people of God we must regain that sense of unity which brought our forebears "into connection." We must develop a clear commitment to work together for the future, with each individual and organization able to see its role in supporting the whole.

The past two hundred years have expanded today's United Methodist Church into a powerful instrument for the accomplishment of God's purpose. Yet it appears that the denomination's effectiveness cannot continue without a new, clear, statement of commitment around which we can rally. This new challenge must help each of us understand what it means to proclaim the faith and to be in service during our third century.

Questions for Consideration

1. What is our task today as individual United Methodists, as local churches, and as a denomination?
2. What must we, as individual Christians and as United Methodists, do to understand and respond to the pressing social issues of today?
3. What characteristics distinguish us as United Methodists from other denominations in the Protestant tradition?
4. What do we wish to affirm about ourselves as United Methodists—for today and for the future?

CHAPTER 2

The Fervent Spirit and Its Fruits

"The spirit of United Methodism was characterized by a zeal for the salvation of sinners, the nurture and edification of believers, and compassion for the powerless, the oppressed, and the dispossessed."[1] Wesley, Asbury, Albright, Otterbein, and their followers became imbued with a fervent spirit and a burning zeal. It was this fervent spirit and the sense of God's assurance which provided their power to witness. In the name of Christ, the people of the assurance went forward to seek out others, regardless of their spiritual or social condition. Let us explore briefly how this power to witness shaped our past and how it can direct our future.

The Power to Witness—The Past

To Proclaim the Faith—The Frontier and the Circuit Rider

What do you do if you firmly believe that God has restored you in faith? How do you respond to those around you who may not understand or share your assurance of God's love and redemption? You tell them about it, of course. It was that simple motivation which fueled the very earliest part of this new Methodist movement. It was witnessing to and proclaiming faith in Jesus Christ!

John Wesley preached in the fields, at the crossroads, and in the churches. The power of that itinerant preaching, driven by a fervent spirit, gave the Wesleyan movement its distinctive character. It was the proclamation of the faith—not liturgies, catechisms, buildings, or organization—that set the tone for early Methodism. The ordained and lay preachers of the movement were known for their witnessing and preaching. In the early years those who heard and received anew the message of the love and assurance of God did two things: They sought to hear more preaching and/or they began to preach themselves.

The earliest preaching was not by ordained ministers. Wesley realized that the message of assurance and perfection could not wait, and because not many ordained clergy were available, "exhorters" and lay preachers began to travel and witness to God's saving power.

As Methodists arrived in and scattered over America, they brought their Wesleyan fervor with them. Their primary concerns were to be nurtured in the faith and to provide vital preaching for others. One reason for the rapid spread of Methodism throughout the new nation was the tenacity with which lay people held to their faith as they moved from place to place. "On many occasions Asbury refers to the migration which he met. In each of these migrations—to the South, to the West, and to the pioneer regions of the North—there were Methodists. Hardly would these Methodist immigrants get settled in their new homes than they would send a request for Methodist preaching."[2]

Lay preachers were largely responsible for the growth of the Methodist movement in many new areas, especially before the arrival of the circuit rider. They proclaimed their faith and witnessed to what it meant in their lives. "'Into newly settled countries, not only as pioneer settlers, but as pioneers of their faith, they have frequently gone, and, in advance of the itinerant preacher, have organized societies, to be transferred afterward to his pastoral care.' Thus, in many places Methodism was well under way before organized Methodism reached the spot."[3]

There were many lay preachers, most of whose names are not recorded. Many of the "exhorters" in the local societies were women. Among the early male lay preachers who traveled widely were Francis Clark in Kentucky, James Foster in South Carolina, and Francis McCormack, who introduced Methodism into Ohio. Harry Hoosier, a black who often traveled with Francis Asbury, also was an eloquent preacher. He and Richard Allen, another black lay preacher, attended the 1784 Christmas Conference, the founding meeting for United Methodism. In

1799, Richard Allen became the first black person to be ordained in the Methodist Episcopal Church. He later helped to organize the African Methodist Episcopal Church.

Another factor in the rapid growth of Methodism was the circuit system of deploying ministers. "Methodism knew no settled ministry. The circuit system could adapt as rapidly as changes necessitated. A circuit on the growing edge of civilization could mother additional circuits as people moved in."[4]

Our predecessors in the faith did not wait until a congregation was developed or a building was constructed. They went in search of people who needed the message. In the first two or three decades following the founding of The Methodist Episcopal Church in 1784, circuits were established so that preachers might be sent to sparsely settled portions of the frontier. The harsh conditions under which the early circuit riders worked to proclaim the faith would be foreign to us today.

> During the entire period many of the Circuits were long, and the Districts covered an extensive territory. Thomas Smith records that at the Conference session in Chestertown, Maryland, in 1805, he was appointed to the Seneca Circuit in the Genesee country of New York, having to travel six hundred miles to reach his field of labor, and that his Circuit was three hundred miles in extent. Elijah Woolsey, appointed in 1803 to take charge of the Albany District, found that the round of the district appointments involved nearly eight hundred miles of travel and an absence from home of between eight and nine weeks. . . . In 1817, John Stewart, appointed to Little Kanawha, in what is now West Virginia, traveled a Circuit five hundred miles in circumference. Some of the appointments were fully forty miles apart over roads that were merely blazed tracks.[5]

Halford Luccock describes the work of the early circuit riders and its heavy toll on their lives. Most died before their work was much more than begun.

> Of the 650 preachers who had joined the Methodist itineracy by the opening of the 19th century, about 500 had to "locate,"

a term that was used for those too worn-out to travel further. Many of the rest had to take periods of recuperation. Others located not because of health, but by reason of lack of support and the desire to marry and establish a home.

Of the first 737 members of the Conferences to die—that is, all who died up to 1847—203 were between 25 and 35 years of age and 121 between 35 and 45. Nearly half died before they were 30 years old. Of 672 of those first preachers whose records we have in full, two-thirds died before they had been able to render 12 years of service. Just one less than 200 died within the first five years. True, there were a few who seemed to be hardened to live to a vigorous old age by the sort of life demanded of the early Methodist preachers. But the majority burned themselves out for God in a few years.[6]

This is our heritage. Why did they do it? Both lay people and clergy proclaimed their faith because they believed in what God had done for them. They preached so that every person could have the opportunity to hear and respond to God's grace. They witnessed with a fervent spirit because they believed that an integral part of their response to God was to go and witness!

To Build the Church—Societies, Classes, and Congregations

Early preachers—both lay and ordained—were charged with responsibility not only to proclaim the faith, but to organize societies and "classes," continuing groups designed for the instruction, growth, and nurture of individual Christians in the faith. These were settings for study and prayer, for discipline, for expressions of mutual concern and love, for encouragement in spiritual growth, and for the channeling of service and outreach to others. "Wesley was too deeply concerned for the ongoing effects of his Movement to be content merely with preaching to great audiences, awakening religious conviction, and influencing people to personal commitment to the Christian life. He knew the re-enforcement of the faith and Christian living that comes from intimate fellowship and the supporting power of organization."[7]

Preaching was before large and small audiences, or congregations. That was the formal setting for hearing about the Christian faith, for worship of God, and for personal commitment. But it was the society—the smaller, more intimate group—where continuing instruction and nurture of the Christian was to be maintained. The society was the arena for the Christian's continuing interaction with other like-minded people.

In 1742 Wesley instituted the "class." Classes were smaller units within societies, established to enable direct personal care for each member. Class leaders were lay people who became a vital core group for Methodism.

In the preamble to the General Rules for societies (still printed in *The Book of Discipline*), we have this statement concerning classes.

That it may the more easily be discerned whether they are indeed working out their own salvation, each society is divided into smaller companies, called **classes,** according to their respective places of abode. There are about twelve persons in a class, one of whom is styled the **leader.** It is his duty:

1. To see each person in his class once a week at least, in order: (1) to inquire how their souls prosper; (2) to advise, reprove, comfort or exhort, as occasion may require; (3) to receive what he is willing to give toward the relief of the preachers, church, and poor.

2. To meet the ministers and the stewards of the society once a week, in order: (1) to inform the minister of any that are sick, or of any that walk disorderly and will not be reproved; (2) to pay the stewards what he has received of his class in the week preceding.[8]

Thus from the very beginning, instruction and guidance were to be available to all members of the society. But it was more than simply instruction. It was the kind of support that only a small group can provide for an individual's spiritual growth. It was the group in which individuals could share the personal struggles of life, temporal as well as spiritual. It was the group that was concerned with proclaiming the faith and making it manifest in the life of the individual. Its purpose was to help the individual move into that more complete relationship with God.

It was assumed, without question, that each member would

share in the society and in the class. "A desire 'to flee from the wrath to come,' expressed in a willingness to submit to the strict discipline prescribed by the General Rules, qualified a person for membership in a society. There was thus constituted a 'hard core' of Methodist people, spiritually alive and joined in mutual trust and helpfulness. From the congregations who heard the Methodist preachers new members were added to the society."[9]

The establishment of societies and classes was a very significant accomplishment of our predecessors in the faith. Not only did those groups provide for growth in spiritual commitment and service through mutual support and encouragement, they also provided leadership training and support for the lay members who held the classes and societies together in the minister's absence.

Through the years the society became what we now call the local church or local congregation. These congregations have stable memberships and have constructed buildings to house worship and other activities. The classes have evolved into church school classes, women's organizations, prayer and study fellowships, and other groups.

The development of the church school movement was another extremely important contribution. In the beginning, only children were included, since adults were presumed to be receiving their instruction in regular classes of the society. At the 1784 Christmas conference, the preachers were asked, "What shall be done for the rising generation?" According to the reply printed in *The Discipline,* "Where there are ten children whose parents are in society, meet with them at least one hour every week." The purpose of the Sunday school was to provide instruction in the Bible and the Christian faith, and it soon became a major point of outreach for both children and adults of the community. It took the form of small, intimate classes in which participants could share their searchings and concerns. In many congregations the Sunday school coexisted with and eventually supplanted the original Wesleyan concept of the class.

As early as the 1870s, articles began to appear in the denomination's magazines, lamenting the decline of class meetings. Indeed in recent years, classes have ceased to provide moral instruction and discipline for the conduct of one's Christian life and are now devoted to study, prayer, and fellowship. In most communities, the ministering of lay members to one another has been diminished by the presence of resident full-time clergy. The responsibility for individual spiritual support and direct inquiry as to other members' spiritual health has been turned over to professional ministers.

Within the membership of the Wesleyan societies and congregations, small groups have been extremely important. They began as places of spiritual guidance, discipline, instruction, encouragement, and comfort. They helped each person find a sense of worth—not only in terms of religious experience, but in terms of his or her place in the total society. Congregations and classes were places of nurture, of learning the Scriptures, of prayer and witnessing. They further served to organize and stimulate social outreach in the community. Guided and instructed by lay leadership, the participants prepared themselves to hear the preaching of clergy, to receive the sacraments, and to be of service to the world.

The congregations and the various groups within them were the chief ways by which the Church was built. Concerns of the faith were shared; broader issues of the denomination were considered and supported there. Congregations within the United Methodist heritage saw themselves not as isolated units, but as parts of the larger entity of which they were a part. More important, the denominations which subsequently joined to form The United Methodist Church saw themselves as a part of the larger Body of Christ. The individual's willingness to repent and receive the grace of God was not an end in itself. Nor was the building up of the local congregations, classes, and subgroups an end in itself. And just as the appropriate response of an individual to God's activity was understood to be the proclaiming of that faith to others, so the congregation came to understand that its obligation was to develop its collective resources to build up the Church—to share, to serve, to proclaim, and to witness.

While the traditional care of our congregational members continues today, it is limited to instruction and loving concern. Lay members' discipline and exhortation of one another no longer occupies a prominent place, as it did in early societies, congregations, classes, and groups. The dynamism to "build the Church" is constrained today because the vision of its meaning is limited largely to the local congregation and its needs—membership, program, and physical plant. Although today church school instruction and much organizational work is still largely in the hands of lay people, the more "religious" functions—prayer instruction, calls for discipleship, proclamation of the faith, and counsel for direction and discipline in the individual's life—are increasingly left to clergy and other professional workers.

To Serve the World

1. *Missions: New Lands and New Congregations.* Strengthened by the knowledge that all persons, whoever and wherever they might be, can be restored in God's love and nurtured in the Christian faith, our forebears believed that as many as possible should hear the gospel message. In this country the work was clear. As the frontiers expanded and the population grew, lay and ordained preachers went forth with the message of God's redemption. This same fervent spirit soon led to consideration of the need to carry the message to other parts of the world.

> Missionary concern, like that for education, was indigenous to Methodism from the beginning, and so expressed itself that, at the Christmas Conference of 1784, Jeremiah Lambert was ordained to work on the island of Antigua, and Freeborn Garrettson and James O. Cromwell were set apart for a mission to Nova Scotia. Indeed, of the thirteen men who received elders' orders at the hands of Wesley's general superintendent, Coke, as the first full accredited Methodist preachers in America, three were sent as missionaries outside the bounds of the United States.[10]

So missionary work was not begun as an afterthought or an appendage; it was central to the key mission—to serve the world as it proclaimed its message. The call to serve was answered by the new denominations being established under the Methodist, Evangelical, and United Brethren banners as soon as their personnel and resources allowed. Extending the ministry to new territories was considered as important as establishing societies and congregations. There was a clear motivation to seek out others in the name of Christ.

In a very real sense, the early circuit riders were missionaries to new and developing lands. The stories are legion of those who responded with vigor to special situations.

John Stewart, of black and American Indian heritage, was converted in a Methodist meeting in 1815. Receiving a strong call, he began to preach among the Wyandot Indians in northern Ohio with Jonathan Pointer, a black who served as his interpreter. His was the first successful and continuing mission in the United Methodist tradition among Native Americans.

In 1837 Ann Wilkins became the first female missionary (other than wives of male missionaries) to be given an assignment outside the United States by the Methodist Episcopal Church. She was sent by the fledgling Missionary Society to teach in Liberia. Much of her support was provided by the new Female Auxiliary to the Missionary Society. Mrs. Wilkins founded the first school for girls outside the United States under the auspices of the Methodist Episcopal Church.

The United Brethren Church developed work in Sierra Leone. Work prospered there in the 1870s under the leadership of Mary and Joseph Green, members of a black United Brethren congregation of Dayton, Ohio.

Isabella Thoburn was sent to India in 1869 as the first missionary of the newly organized Women's Foreign Missionary Society of the Methodist Episcopal Church. Her work included the development of the first Christian college for women in the Orient.

World outreach in the mission of the church during the latter part of the nineteenth century was amazing. At the time of the centenary of the church in 1884, there were twenty-four annual conferences and mission conferences in China, India, Europe, Africa, South America, Japan, Korea, Malaysia, and Mexico. The missionary task involved not only preaching the gospel but also building churches, founding schools, establishing hospitals, and planning strategy for occupying as large an area of the entire field as humanly possible and placing the distinctive stamp of Methodism on every phase of the program.[11]

Our forebears in the faith did not serve only their own needs; they felt compelled to reach out. They reached out to those immediately around them; they sought to bring the message of Christ to the whole nation; and they sensed a call and responsibility to send as many persons as possible to all parts of the world. Congregations and organizations were developed in the United States in order to enable the message of Christ to be spread more effectively. It was a compellingly simple task—proclaim and serve.

2. *The Struggle Against Injustice.* We have spoken of the early Methodists' sense of assurance of God's salvation and of their belief that all persons can move toward perfection in love. These twin emphases provided the motivation for forceful witnessing to God's love and grace, and also for addressing the social ills of any society in which the Christian lived. "Whatever one's attitude toward the expediency of a man's claiming that he had been made perfect in love (and Wesley never did so for himself), one cannot help seeing how his insistence on the doctrines of assurance and of Christian perfection would generate a pervasive sense of social responsibility, and a tremendous dynamic for the relief of suffering men, as well as for the reform of the abuses that made them suffer."[12]

One of Wesley's first injunctions to those "in connection" with him was to care for the poor. This was not merely a matter of collecting funds for relief. It involved direct personal care, visits to prisoners, and attempts to change the uncaring nature of social, economic, and legal systems. "Admittedly [Wesley's] primary objective was to preach the gospel of repentance and salvation to individuals. But his precept and example alike give convincing demonstration that he was interested not only in the heavenly Kingdom for which he would prepare men's souls, but also in the society in which their minds and bodies lived on earth."[13]

So the followers of Wesley, Asbury, Otterbein, Boehm, and Albright found themselves not only witnessing to the power of God's grace but dealing with the social issues and concerns of their times. Let us illustrate with only a few of the major social struggles waged in our nation's history.

The issue of racism has been intertwined with the

development of United Methodism from the very beginning. Blacks were a part of the earliest societies in this nation, but their status was considered to be lower than that of white members. In fact, some blacks were slaves of the white members. As early as 1786 in the St. George congregation in Philadelphia, tensions had arisen over the manner in which blacks were treated, and similar difficulties arose in Methodist congregations in other cities. In 1787 Richard Allen established a separate congregation for blacks in Philadelphia; Daniel Coker did the same in Baltimore; and in 1816 Allen invited black leaders related to the Methodist movement to join in the establishment of a separate organization. Thus the African Methodist Episcopal Church was founded.

The race issue focused in the slavery dispute that was to separate both the church and the nation. The Methodist Episcopal Church, with a broad constituency in both northern and southern states, actively debated the issue throughout the early part of the nineteenth century. The issue finally divided the denomination in 1844, sixteen years before it brought the nation itself to war. In the present century, the issue of racism has continued to confront the denomination in its formal organizational life as well as in society as a whole. While The United Methodist Church has not yet achieved perfection either for itself or for society, the denomination affirms its belief in the equality of all and is struggling to find that perfection in love for all persons.

Viewing alcohol abuse as one of the major social evils of the nation, our forebears in the faith marshaled their resources to direct people away from alcohol, and even to remove it from society. This struggle became formalized in the temperance movement, which experienced its greatest strength in the late nineteenth and early twentieth centuries. The Prohibition Amendment to the Constitution of the United States was a direct result of intense activity by Evangelicals, United Brethren, and Methodists, who joined with others to bring about this change. Although the legal prohibition did not remain in effect long, United Methodism still maintains a strong position against the misuse of alcohol.

United Methodism has addressed many other social

concerns and issues in the course of its history. Peace, social justice, suffrage, labor reform, women's rights, and the self-development of peoples are but a few of the social issues that have occupied the attention and energies of the denomination. Leadership on many of these issues came from the women of the church and their organizations. "In all branches of Methodism, women have been at the forefront of those concerned about social issues. They gave early support to issues of suffrage, temperance, and race. They have engaged in practical work in inner city and rural community centers as well as with women's and children's rights."[14]

What motivated this involvement in social issues? *It was the intense concern for the well-being of the individual—each person—in this world and in the next.* It was a conviction that there is potential for improvement in the life of *every* person. In order to realize this potential, the Christian is *obligated* to address the social, economic, and political issues that work against the religious, personal, and social development of the individual!

To serve the world, then, is part of the obligation of the Christian. Wesley's followers believed that the responsibilities of being a Christian include not only proclaiming the faith, but seeking to redress injustices that would hinder the full growth of each person. This type of service has not been easily or readily understood by all—not even by those within the denomination itself. Yet the history of United Methodism has been one of Christians who seek to serve the world in the name of Christ.

The call to be in service to the world has manifested itself in ways other than in the confrontation of major social issues. Originally, it involved alleviating the physical needs of the poor as well as restoring their sense of worth and dignity. Its focus expanded to include striving to be of help whatever the circumstance, and many forms of ministry resulted. Community centers, established to serve a variety of needs in both rural and urban areas, helped the immigrant masses to become accustomed to American life. Education was provided for those who might not otherwise have had such opportunities. The denomination has sought to serve people from various nations with churches, education, and a range of social services. In addition to English- and German-speaking groups of immigrants, it has served persons from Italy, Norway, Sweden, Finland, Eastern Europe, Japan, and the Philippines. In more recent times the denomination has sought to assist those arriving from South and Latin America, Korea, Southeast Asia, and the South Pacific, in terms of their faith commitment and their individual needs. Other aspects of the denomination's outreach program include the fields of health care, needs of the aged, and special services for children and youth.

While the services mentioned have been established to provide skilled assistance to those in need, let us not forget the innumerable acts of Christian love and charity performed quietly on a person-to-person basis by concerned United Methodists. The call is to be of service, and the response may be a simple gesture of love for another at a particular time of need. Whatever its form, we must remember that *we are called to service as part of the way we proclaim our faith.*

The Power to Witness—The Future

Our United Methodist forebears discovered the power to witness and affirm the future as they saw it. They perceived that their restored relationship with God could make a significant difference in their hearts. With that conviction came the power to act, in their own lives and in their society. This power enabled them to proclaim the faith to others, even at the risk of not being understood or accepted. It enabled them to take the message of the redeeming love of God outside the church to persons in spiritual and social need, wherever they were to be found.

Although the United Brethren, Evangelical, and Methodist fellowships had different points of origin, their beginnings were closely interrelated. Each quickly developed a clear understanding of purpose, both for their organizations and for the individuals involved. The call was to receive God's blessing and to take that message in service to others.

The movement's purpose, as expressed by John Wesley, was adopted officially by the Methodist Episcopal Church at its 1785 conference. That purpose was "to reform the nation and

spread Scriptural holiness throughout the land." This statement represents our heritage. We receive it and rejoice in it.
Although our history has not been without failures and
tensions, a great legacy is ours. Yet we cannot simply reflect on
our past. Where shall we turn to find the power to witness and
affirm our Christian faith in the future?

The Power of Spiritual Conviction

The Christian message still affirms the individual. We must
rediscover the Wesleyan assurance of God's grace for our lives.
Acceptance of this assurance must come first. It is our starting
point.

With new strength, we must emphasize our affirmation that
through the grace of God freely given to us in Jesus Christ, we
are indeed forgiven and restored to God. In this assurance that
we are sought and loved, we find both our comfort in God and
our motivation to respond. The traditional words of the
invitation in the Sacrament of Holy Communion state it: "Ye
that do truly and earnestly repent of your sins . . . draw near
with faith."

Through the years, both as a denomination and as
individuals, we seem to have lost a sense of the power of
spiritual conviction. Many of us are hesitant to affirm our faith
commitment; we fail to understand what this means in the
context of our identity as United Methodists. Many of us limit
expressions of our religious convictions to formal church-
related situations. Prayers at meetings are often quite
perfunctory. We frequently hide our deep personal feelings
and religious convictions behind the veneer of formal and
impersonal customs we have developed.

In the complexities of today's world, we become preoccupied
with matters other than our spiritual life. Opportunities for
recreation and pleasure are almost unlimited, and as we
become caught up in the many conflicting demands for our
time and energies, our Christian convictions become sub-
merged in other concerns. It is hard for us to perceive how we
may have much impact on our own lives or on the lives of
others. Our contemporary society makes it more and more

difficult to suggest to others or to ourselves that the key ingredient in our lives is our relationship with God.

We must reaffirm the transforming power available to us through repentance and faith. Wesley, Asbury, Otterbein, Albright, and those "in connection" with them testified first to their personal spiritual experiences. They were not perfect in the faith, but they affirmed that it was possible to grow more and more toward a perfect relationship in love with God and with one another. This is the spiritual conviction that drove them and that can draw us to the limits of our energies in seeking and serving others in the name of Christ. Further, it provides a context for our understanding of and response to the future.

Does the power and dynamism of spiritual conviction lie largely dormant in many of our members, and in the denomination as a whole? Perhaps we assume the presence of spiritual conviction, but are too reserved to discuss it. Perhaps we are hesitant to be too vocal, lest we find ourselves conspicuously different from many about us. Perhaps we discuss the great issues without understanding or compassion for the individuals affected by those issues. Perhaps as individuals and as a denomination, we have indeed lost much of the driving conviction behind our spiritual affirmations!

These thoughts raise serious questions for us as individuals and as a church. How deep, how strong is the base of spiritual conviction from which we will attempt to move into service in the future? How do we see ourselves in relation to God? What must we do, then, as individuals and as a denomination, to proclaim the faith and serve more effectively?

Many of the great hymns reflect a sense of personal assurance in the faith. They express inner feelings of conviction that God has acted and that we must also act in God's name. Think of some of the hymns of that era: "Blessed Assurance, Jesus Is Mine," "There Is a Balm in Gilead," "Amazing Grace, How Sweet the Sound." The same feelings are expressed in Charles Wesley's hymn "O How Happy Are They."

> O how happy are they
> Who the Savior obey,

And have laid up their treasure above!
Tongue can never express
The sweet comfort and peace
Of a soul in its earliest love.

That sweet comfort was mine,
When the favor divine
I first found in the blood of the Lamb;
When my heart first believed,
What a joy I received,
What a heaven in Jesus's name! . . .

Now my remnant of days
Would I speak of his praise
Who hath died my poor soul to redeem.
Whether many or few,
All my years are his due;
May they all be devoted to him.[15]

When we understand our personal relationship to God, we will find our course for the future as Christians. The focus and purpose of all our activities in Christ's name are intimately intertwined with our understanding of what God has done in our lives and what God can do in others' lives. Our spiritual convictions will empower us to serve by translating our faith experience into action.

This power will be given not only to individuals but to the denomination. Yet we cannot assume a spiritual base for the denomination; we must reexamine the reason we join together under the banner of United Methodism. Surely it is more than mere custom or convenience. We must combine our individual spiritual convictions to provide cogent and meaningful expressions of prayer, concern, healing, and action. The spiritual base from which we move must be understood clearly, stated clearly, and witnessed to effectively, if it is to commend itself to others.

We must let people everywhere know that we who call ourselves United Methodists move from a ground swell of spiritual conviction, not relying only on momentum and resources accumulated in the past. We must give clear evidence that we seek to serve God—not to be bigger or more powerful or to preserve what we have developed in the past, but because our calling as redeemed, restored people requires us to proclaim and serve.

Some have said that as a denomination, we are adrift—that we are doing many mighty deeds, but without a clear sense of the rationale behind our actions; that we are preoccupied with many activities, but without a clear knowledge of the reasons for expending our energies and resources; that we administer the past without a clear perception of the future. How shall we respond to such critics? What evidence can we gather to respond to such statements?

As a people of the assurance, we shall move with resolve and vigor only if we have some clear sense of who we are. Our future as United Methodists will depend on the strength of our spiritual conviction that God has acted on behalf of all persons; that all persons may move into a more complete relationship with God and with others. Our future will depend on the strength of our conviction that we as individuals and as a denomination can work in this world to address spiritual and human needs. Our ability to proclaim the faith as United Methodists will depend on our ability to communicate clearly to those about us that God is at work in our lives and in our church.

The Power of Prayer, Study, and Discipline

In addition to preaching and witnessing, early United Methodists understood the need for each person to come into close association with other Christians for prayer, for study of the Scriptures, and for guidance and mutual assistance.

These activities have received less emphasis in recent times. We have lost much of our power to proclaim and serve, because our witness and service are not adequately undergirded with prayer and study. Many of our members do not engage in regular Bible study or devotional activity. Therefore they are not well informed about the content of their faith, and their personal spiritual disciplines are not well developed. Apart from the main preaching/worship service in the local church, most gatherings of adult members in our churches tend to center on business, social, or organizational matters. Most of our members do not participate in adult church school classes. Prayer fellowships have largely disappeared. Few churches still offer Wednesday night opportunities for study and prayer. The one major group that has retained an emphasis on study and prayer is United Methodist Women.

Further, as a denomination, we are leaving the nurture of one another in the faith to only a very few—generally the pastor and other employed church staff, church school teachers, and a very limited number of others. We have increasingly assumed that Christian nurture is the job of professionally trained people. As a consequence, the vast majority of lay people have withdrawn from this type of activity for adults. We have fewer and fewer settings in which to meet together for prayer, mutual guidance, and assistance in growing in Christian love and perfection.

When do we have an occasion to come together to lift spiritual and other concerns we have for one another? When do we have an occasion to study the Scriptures together, to develop our prayer and devotional life, to learn of our United Methodist heritage, to understand the issues and concerns in the world that require our response? In what arenas can we learn how to best serve in God's name?

The need for study and growth in our Christian faith is ever present. We need continual opportunities to explore in detail, in the company of others, the riches of the Scriptures. Such opportunities help us to understand the continuing revelations of God and the faith we seek to proclaim. Through prayer, we come to a greater appreciation of God's will for us. Through study of our heritage, we learn of the strengths and values of our life together as United Methodists.

Concerted study, nurture, and prayer among members are major sources of strength in the development of Christian understanding and convictions. Yet increasingly, United Methodists perceive themselves as primarily members of a worshiping community (on Sunday morning) rather than as active participants. Thus we have lost much of the driving edge of the denomination.

We must be more involved in groups where we can share our

experiences as developing Christians. We must take advantage of the opportunities that are available to explore with others the richness of prayer life and our spiritual journeys. There Christians can share their faith experiences, disappointments and trials, triumphs and successes. This type of study and nurture fosters a power that informs and strengthens, that gives direction to individuals, to local congregations, and to the entire denomination. To our intense surprise, how extraordinary would be the power developed, channeled, and released from hundreds—indeed, thousands—of clusters of United Methodist groups gathered to understand God's will and marshaled to go forth in Christ's name!

The Power of Action in Service

United Methodism has had a long tradition of living out its faith in action and service. One of the first steps taken by the earliest members of our movement involved outreach to the poor and dispossessed. With the compulsion to proclaim the faith, came the drive to be of service and to deal with the significant issues of human need and development. During our first two hundred years, we have focused on winning people to Christ and improving the lives of those in need.

We greatly appreciate the value of concerted action. United Methodists are at the forefront of many organizations, associations, and activities. We have been leaders of crucial positions on many important social issues. We have developed significant educational and health-and-welfare programs, and organizations through which to serve persons at their time of need.

Now we are uncertain about our directions for future actions. Many major projects and institutions are being reevaluated in terms of their primary functions. As world and national conditions change rapidly, we struggle to remain relevant in our service. The United Methodist Church has undertaken so many tasks that we often have difficulty keeping track of them all. We cannot fully comprehend all that is being done, nor can we accurately gauge the effectiveness and continuing need for all the activities in which we are engaged.

When we do not understand the primary objectives for many

of our activities, we wonder whether the power for action and the desire for continuance derives from spiritual conviction, or from misguided desires to continue activities or institutions simply because they have had an honorable past. One wonders if perhaps, in supporting these myriad activities, we have drawn upon our spiritual reserves to such a degree that the depth of our commitment has been depleted.

There is no question that we as United Methodists will be at work in the future. What is becoming increasingly clear, however, is that we must once again understand the reasons for our service and the motivations for our actions. *Power for our action must derive from our convictions regarding our faith and from the nurture that faith receives in prayer and study.* Only then can we describe with clarity both the reasons for our service and action, and the actions themselves. We must simultaneously reexamine our faith commitment and our motivations for putting that faith into action in the types of service we choose to provide.

The Power to Form the Future

We are uniquely the people of the assurance and of the belief that we can move on to perfection. Both these concepts affirm the present and provide our hope and purpose for the future. "The new heaven and new earth" are possible. Our founders, who understood these concepts, developed an ability to act for the conversion of individuals and for the reform of society.

The historical growth and expansion by our forebears—in this nation and throughout the world—resulted from the power of those who sought others in the name of Christ. There was a singularity of purpose. Admittedly, there were tensions and differences as to how this could be accomplished, but the primary thrust was clearly identifiable.

In recent decades our primary thrust has not been as readily apparent. United Methodists have accommodated to their society in may ways. Although we are still active in service, action, and reform, our shared base of spiritual conviction is not always obvious, and the source or strength of conviction that will guide United Methodism in the future is not clear. Consequently, much available energy is not used effectively, and much of the motivating power is lost.

Colin Williams has put it this way: "The concern [is] that the modernising process . . . has left us floundering and directionless. It is not just that as a result of the loss of faith we are rich in things, but poor in soul. It is also that being poor in soul, we are now endangering the things as well since the inner decay in our culture has left us with no clear sense of purpose."[16] In many ways Williams' statement about the American culture in general reflects the condition of United Methodism in particular. Until the mid-1960s, we had moved through a long period of growth and success. At about 1965, we reached a peak in recorded membership and attendance. There was a high level of consensus about what needed to be done and how to accomplish those tasks.

Today, however, we are discovering that as a denomination we are no longer able to do all the things we did before; we cannot continue to enjoy all the luxuries we formerly shared. Our resources are more limited than the tasks we believe must be undertaken. United Methodism must make some hard and crucial decisions. Yet we do not sense the presence of the power or wisdom to reflect on our options and move into the future with vigor. Perhaps in becoming rich in things, we have indeed become poor in soul. Even so, we know that it is the power of the soul that ultimately brings about changes in individuals and in society.

We will receive our power to make a significant and successful impact on the future when we develop a clear understanding of who we are as a people of God. We will rediscover the strengths that can be ours when we renew our own personal relationships with God and join together with other United Methodists. The power for all that we do and can become will arise from our assurance that we are now restored to God, that we have been called to respond to God's grace through worship, proclamation, and service, and that individually and collectively, we can not only bring others into the same reconciling relationship, but can act to bring about significant changes in persons and society. Our power is of God. Channeled through our lives, it is seen in our sense of commitment to act on behalf of the future.

In the next four chapters, we will explore the meaning of the power of spiritual conviction for proclamation, nurture, and action. We will view this power in the light of God's continuing grace in our lives and in light of our response, both as individuals and as The United Methodist Church.

Questions for Consideration

1. If we firmly believe that God has restored us in love and mercy, how can we share this sense of assurance with others?
2. What motivated lay people and ministers of the early United Methodist heritage to share their faith? What motivates us?
3. How do we provide the nurture and support for one another that enables each person to grow in God's grace and move toward perfection in love?
4. How can we as individuals, as congregations, and as a denomination develop the power to proclaim the faith and to serve others in God's name?

CHAPTER 3

A Vital Piety

The starting point for whatever we do as Christians and as United Methodists is our own faith commitment to Jesus Christ. To use a phrase that has been very much a part of United Methodist tradition, all that we do must begin with "a vital piety." Let us explore the meaning of this vital piety for us, as individual Christians.

A Vital Piety—As an Individual

The Christian faith has always been a highly personal one. Jesus spoke to the individual who needed to be restored in love to God. He also said that the individual should respond to other persons in terms of their needs. And while he did not focus on the major social institutions of his time, his teachings did carry clear ramifications for those institutions.

Jesus spoke to the personal needs of those he taught. He urged people to repent, to receive the grace of God through faith, and to respond in love to God and to others around them. Both their faith and their resulting active response were of great importance. That response was not to be passive, reflected merely through participation in certain rituals or through following certain narrow rules. Their faith was to engage their whole beings in loving response. It was, indeed, *a vital piety*, focusing attention on God and on the Christian's response in love and service to others, enabled by God through grace.

We stand as a part of the Protestant tradition, which began with the struggle to show that vital piety did not depend on a priest or on the sacraments as the sole channels of God's grace.

The Protestant Reformation enlarged many people's under-standing of the Christian faith. It emphasized that God's love is constantly available, if we will only engage in an active search for that love. The Scriptures are available to all of us, and we need only make our commitment to Christ in repentance and faith to find the assurance of God's reconciliation and love.

By the time of our United Methodist founders, active faith commitment and response to God were obscured by the formalities of established, liturgy-oriented churches. The German Lutheran, the German Reformed churches, and the Church of England, as well as the Catholic Church, relied heavily upon the sacraments, the liturgy, and the priest to be the primary channels of God's grace. For some, this was a very helpful expression of Christianity. But it tended to place more emphasis on careful observance of form, correct phrasing of ritual, and approved creeds and confessional statements than on the personal experience of the individual Christian.

Otterbein, though a German Reformed pastor all his adult life, understood the need for a strong personal affirmation and response to the Christian message. Albright, though unlet-tered, stressed the need for the individual to embrace whole-heartedly the Christian faith in his or her life and to live out the implications of that faith daily. John Wesley, a priest of the Church of England, realized that the faith needs of many were not being met in the established church. All three clearly saw that we must respond to God with complete repentance and with a commitment to "lead a new life, following the commandments of God." This is a vital piety, focusing on our response to God's grace through repentance and love.

John Wesley wrote a description of a follower, seeking to explain those who were a part of his movement. In "The Character of a Methodist" he defined the nature of a Methodist.

"A Methodist is one who has the love of God shed abroad in his heart by the Holy Ghost given unto him"; one who "loves the Lord his God with all his heart, and with all his soul, and with all his mind, and with all his strength." God is the joy of his heart and the desire of his soul, which is constantly crying out,

"Whom have I in heaven but thee? and there is none upon earth that I desire beside thee! My God and my all! Thou art the strength of my heart, and my portion forever!"[1]

Wesley then explained that this commitment involves an active participation in the hope of salvation, in prayer, and in living in right relationship with God and neighbor. We are to be known by the fruits of our actions, which issue forth from this vital piety. Wesley closed with this point:

> As he has time he "does good unto all men," unto neighbors and strangers, friends and enemies; and that in every possible kind, not only to the bodies by "feeding the hungry, clothing the naked, visiting those that are sick or in prison," but much more does he labor to do good to their souls as of the ability which God giveth, to awaken those that sleep in death; to bring those who are awakened to the atoning blood that, "being justified by faith, they may have peace with God," and to provoke those who have peace with God to abound more in love and good works. And he is willing to "spend and be spent herein" . . . so that they may "all come unto the measure of the stature of the fullness of Christ."[2]

Each of us must be deeply committed in our personal response to God and in our outreach to others. This is a faith that is neither narrow, nor exclusive, nor rigidly prescribed. It is a faith that is open, responding, and vital. This has been the nature of our United Methodist heritage. We seek first that assurance in the faith, and then we look for ways to respond.

How Are We Informed in This Vital Piety?

Each of us is called to make our own personal commitment to God. As we engage in the study of our faith—and as we assist others in their spiritual growth—how are we to be guided in "going on to perfection"? We will come to understand the meaning of a vital piety within the context of some boundaries. While our faith commitment is a personal one, uniquely entered into, our interpretations and understandings of Christian faith are not free to run unbridled in any direction.

Our heritage has provided us with guidelines to inform our

personal religious experience and to channel our responses to God's grace. In addition to the personal experience of the risen Christ, other major factors combine to nurture us as we affirm and strengthen our vital piety. These key factors influence and give direction to the development and understanding of our theology. In our tradition we have come to understand four primary interconnected guidelines for our Christian faith: Scripture, tradition, experience, and reason.

1. *Scripture.* The Bible is our source of information concerning our faith. "Scripture is the primary source and guideline for doctrine. The Bible is the deposit of a unique testimony to God's self-disclosures: in the world's creation, redemption and final fulfillment; in Jesus Christ as the incarnation of God's Word; in the Holy Spirit's constant activity in the dramas of history."[3]

We cannot develop our personal faith without constantly reading and referring to God's witness in the Bible. One of our first acts of response as Christians must be to inform ourselves through the Scriptures. It is our task to understand how God in Christ has acted in our lives and in the world. "To embrace *Scriptures* as a primary standard for our theology is to acknowledge that, in the events recounted therein, we find the determinative clues about the meaning of our lives. Since Jesus Christ is the center of the biblical revelation, other events of the Bible are interpreted through their relationship to him."[4]

2. *Tradition.* We also learn about our faith through tradition. We observe what others have said and done as part of their response in faith to God. We read the testimony of other Christians who helped form our understandings of the Christian Church and its struggles in the past and today. The role of tradition in our understanding of our faith is well described by Neal Fisher:

> It was out of the earliest traditions that significant portions of the Bible were formed, and it is partly out of the study and proclamation of each generation that our current under-standing of the Bible is formed. Each generation of Christians has sought to express the truth of faith in terms appropriate to its own situation. We are free, and obliged, to learn from their

discovery. We should not assume that a new idea, by virtue of its newness, is superior in its insight to the old.[5]

Traditions we share within The United Methodist Church differ from those of other denominations in forms of church government and customs. Yet we can be informed by those traditions also and remain open to ideas that commend themselves as central to the Christian faith. We learn from others as we seek to grow and develop our own faith.

3. *Experience.* The third aspect is our own experience—our own unique awareness of what God has done for us and the response that we individually can and must make. As each individual is unique, so our experiences in relation to God are unique. As we understand the distinctive character of our own faith response, we must seek to understand the responses of others as well.

To recognize that each person's experience is different is not to imply that we all live and respond in isolation. Our experience is to be shared with rejoicing, even as we share in the joy of the Christian experiences of others. "Christian experience is not only deeply private and inward; it is also corporate and active. The Bible knows nothing of solitary religion. God's gift of liberating love must be shared if it is to survive."[6] So it is that both our own personal experience and that of others inform us in the development of a vital piety.

4. *Reason.* Finally, we must apply reason to our faith. We must reflect upon what we read and experience. We must bring together the Scriptures, the traditions, the realities of the world around us, and our own experiences to develop a cogent vision of our Christian faith, for ourselves and for others as well. That which seems unclear must be clarified. Those things that are not essential to the core of Christian experience must be identified so that we can concentrate on only the essentials. This is the task of reason. If we understand our faith well, we can more easily share it with others. "Reason is employed in the communication of the Gospel, phrasing its message in the most cogent, thoughtful terms the believer is capable of."[7]

With our commitment to God comes the need to understand, to discover the truths that have come to us through the ages, to search the biblical record for greater understanding of God's revelation. Our vital piety is nurtured as we seek to learn more of the meaning of God's action in our lives and in the lives of others. Scripture, tradition, experience, and reason inform us so that our commitment may be stronger and our response to God's action be in accordance with God's will. It is through this commitment and nurture that we come to understand the requirements for action and service which are the natural outgrowths of a vital piety.

To Be Among the People Called United Methodists

Our first step in the Christian faith is to discover our own relationship with God through Christ, expressed in our own vital piety, or faith. We grow in our faith as we study the Scriptures and develop our prayer life. We grow further as we join in worship and service.

Thus at some point in our faith journey, we choose to come together with other Christians. We voluntarily join the Church in one of its many forms or branches. As Robert L. Wilson puts it: "A fundamental fact of every local church in America is that it is a voluntary organization. People participate and give their time and money because the church is important to them. No one is required to be a member of a church. If any person is unhappy with a particular congregation, he or she may seek another or drop out altogether."[8]

As United Methodists, we made a conscious decision to join others who are a part of the United Methodist heritage. Many of us were raised in the denomination: We worshiped with our families in the same congregations for many years, and we joined the church as a part of a church school confirmation class when we confessed our faith. Many of us transferred into our present local church from another United Methodist congregation. But others left backgrounds in other denominations, and some became a part of a United Methodist congregation by confession of faith. Whatever our backgrounds, whatever our immediate reason—convenience, conviction, warmth of fellowship—we all have chosen, at some point, to share in our Christian journey with the people of the assurance, United Methodists. We choose to remain a part of this expression of the Christian Church.

Our congregations are the contemporary Wesleyan societies. Wesley described a society as a company of persons "having the *form* and seeking the *power* of godliness, united in order to pray together, to receive the word of exhortation, and to watch over one another in love, that they may help each other to work out their salvation."[9] We gather to share with one another our experiences in the Christian faith. We come together to hear and participate in the proclamation of the faith, to study and grow in our understanding of God's continuing action, and to act and serve in response to God's love.

When we join The United Methodist Church, we are asked first to affirm our acceptance of Jesus Christ as Savior. This public profession of our faith is a crucial step. It makes known to the congregation that we do indeed accept Christ and have received the assurance of God's grace. More than that, it causes us to publicly declare our faith in Christ, to make our personal decision and commitment known to the assembled community of Christians. Following this affirmation, we confirm that we have received and do profess the Christian faith as contained in the Scriptures and that we promise anew to live a Christian life. These are our primary affirmations and the keystones of our own personal faith.

Only after answering these questions, are we asked specifically about our denomination. "Will you be loyal to The United Methodist Church, and uphold it by your prayers, your presence, your gifts, and your service?" By our previous answers, we proclaimed our faith as Christians. This question allows us to make known our desire to become a part of The United Methodist Church, to share in its traditions, its sense of response to God's action, and its fellowship. The local congregation receives us into membership on behalf of the total denomination. We become members, not just of the local church where we recite the membership vows, but of the entire denomination. By declaring our faith in Jesus Christ and our intent to be among the people known as United Methodists, we become part of the total worldwide life and work of the denomination.

In the local congregation we have our most immediate experiences in the Christian community. But we are also a part of the worldwide communion of United Methodists, at work to proclaim and to serve in the name of Christ. Both the local church and the total denomination assist and inform us in sharing our faith, nurture us through study and prayer, and provide channels for service and outreach to others. It is an extraordinary relationship, one which all of us have entered because of our response to God in Christ and our own desire to be at work in the world with like-minded Christians.

The Commitment to Act

When we accepted Christ as our Savior, we accepted the obligation to respond. We received the assurance of God's grace, but we also received the instruction that we are to share this assurance with others. We are to grow in our faith so that we become better prepared to serve in God's name. Our acceptance of Christ cannot be passive—it must involve a commitment to act.

When we chose to become United Methodists, we assumed a further obligation to respond. We became a part of a community of faith. In the local congregation, we are to share our faith experiences, pray together, and provide mutual guidance, comfort, and encouragement. We are to gather for study of the Scriptures and to learn of our Christian faith and heritage. We are to search for avenues to be of service to others. Many of these activities will be within the context of those developed and supported primarily by United Methodists; in some, we will join other Christians in ecumenical and cooperative settings to carry forward our witness and service.

The United Methodist heritage has been one of proclamation, nurture, and service. We are challenged to become active Christians within this denomination, which we affirm with our presence, our prayers, our gifts, and our service. United Methodist tradition has always included a vital piety, involved in creative activity to bring others into a saving relationship with God and to meet their spiritual and human needs. Our acceptance of United Methodist membership and responsibility cannot be merely passive. We must commit ourselves to act.

A Vital Piety—With Others as United Methodists

A Commitment to the Connection

There is a United Methodist term which describes the bond that unites or holds our denomination together. We call it "the connection." This means that all the components of the denomination—members, ministers, local churches, annual conferences, General Conference, boards, agencies, and institutions—all are related to one another in a vital and significant way. This is a unique organizational style. Ours is not a denomination of independent or autonomous congregations which communicate with one another only as they elect to do so. Nor is ours a denomination governed by a strong central authority. United Methodists are held together by our desire to be "in connection" with one another. The phrase comes from John Wesley. His early followers did not join one organization or leave another. They elected to be "in connection" with Wesley, to associate with him in extending his work. It was an individual's voluntary act to enter that relationship.

The primary organizational aspect of the United Methodist connection is the annual conference. Initially its membership consisted solely of ministers "in connection" with Wesley. In the United States, the annual conference of the Methodist Episcopal Church was designed to plan for preaching and outreach, for assignment of clergy to their tasks, and for consideration of other general concerns. The Church of the United Brethren in Christ and the Evangelical Association, which adopted the Methodist style of organization, also developed annual conference organizations. Thus the annual conference, a unique creation of John Wesley, brought "into connection" with one another those who agreed with Wesley's emphases and who set about to support one another in proclaiming the faith.

Today annual conference membership consists of an equal number of lay and clergy persons from local churches within the geographic boundaries of the conference. In addition to dealing with a broad range of topics, it establishes the program and financial undergirdings for the coordinated ministry of its congregations and members. Over the course of years, annual conferences have delegated to the General Conference the responsibility for establishing specific policies for all conferences "in the connection."

The annual conference also delegates responsibilities to local churches within its boundaries. Local United Methodist congregations are not separate and autonomous from the conference, but rather exist in connection with all local churches in the conference. Pastors are not members of local congregations which they serve, but of the annual conference. Indeed, even the property of a local church is held in trust by the local congregation for The United Methodist Church, and is subject to the provisions of *The Book of Discipline.* We are bound to one another as congregations, members, and ministers "in the connection."

While local congregations do serve their local communities, they also are involved in the broader concerns of the annual conference and the total denomination. No congregation stands alone. It is supported by and supports the life and work of the annual conference and all of United Methodism. We share in the major programs and direction of the whole. The training of clergy is partially underwritten by the entire denomination. The annual conference certifies the training and competency of persons for ministry; bishops assign ministers to local churches in view of the needs of local congregations and ministers, but also on behalf of the total connection.

This is the unique way in which The United Methodist Church functions. There is a bond between all local churches, and there is a bond between the local church, the annual conference, and the General Conference. All "in the connection," at all levels, seek to develop an effective and significant ministry.

What does this mean to us as individuals? First, each of us, responding in faith to God, made the decision to become a Christian and to grow in understanding of our faith. Second, each of us elected to become part of a fellowship of Christian believers. We joined others who had previously come together as United Methodists. In effect, when we chose to become

United Methodists, we joined "in connection" with millions of others who had, at some time, made a similar decision. We became a part not only of the fellowship of the local congregation, but of United Methodism as a whole.

In our own personal Christian experience, we are supported by many programs and services of both the local congregation and the total denomination. In the local church we find avenues for expressing and strengthening our faith commitment to Christ and for devoting our energies and resources in service. We ourselves may not need all the programs, activities, and services made available by the local church and the denomination—we may not even agree with the programs developed; yet we recognize that others may need these to fulfill their Christian commitment. And even though we may not be aware of all that is being done throughout United Methodism, we are willing to help support these ministries through our prayers and gifts. We do this because we are "in connection" with one another to proclaim and to serve, committed to journey with others who have made the same choice. Together we merge our commitments to strengthen God's kingdom in whatever way we can. We make a commitment "to the connection," to strive together to express our own vital piety.

So we are in connection, in our theological perspective and in the organizational ties that bind us together. We are in connection in the mutual care and support we provide one another in the local congregation, in the training and deployment of ministers, and in the support of service ministries in the community, the nation, and the world. Randolph Nugent, general secretary of our General Board of Global Ministries, stated that "the connection is the unity which makes possible the mission." It is through being in connection with one another that we discover a common purpose and direction for accomplishing our tasks. It is through being in connection that we find the strength of commitment and the resources to undertake a wide range of ministries and service. It is "in connection" that we find the power, regardless of the setting, to proclaim the faith, build the Church, and serve the world.

Together into the Future

We make our faith commitments as individuals. We begin to express these within the context of the Christian community. We choose to be "in connection" with other United Methodists for proclamation and service. We recognize that when our personal witness is blended with that of others, the sum of our efforts is greater than the total of the individual parts, and we sense the power that lies behind that corporate witness.

We have inherited that kind of witness. It was our United Methodist forebears, in connection with one another, who reviewed the qualifications of the clergy who were to serve in the new land. It was they who provided the resources, however limited, which sent the early lay preachers and circuit riders into frontier communities. It was they who established printing facilities, so that laity and clergy could have books and other study resources. It was they who saw the need to send missionaries throughout the world.

What lies behind this kind of corporate witness? It begins when individuals enter into prayer and study for the growth and development of their own personal faith. The very presence of one professing Christian may be all that is needed to influence another. It begins when individuals seek ways to personally extend the ministry of Christ through their own actions. It begins when individuals come together to share their time and resources. As we join with others in classes, congregations, conferences, and the total church, we transform our own personal vital piety into the spiritual conviction of collective power. This is the uniqueness of our United Methodist tradition: We have a personal commitment to a vital piety which speaks to each of us; we also have a collective commitment to witness to Christ and his kingdom.

Now is the time to reflect not only on the past, but also and especially on the years ahead. What is our potential for Christian witness in the future? How are we to mobilize the energies that grow out of our personal lives, energies that will be channeled through our local churches and the denomination? What is God calling us to do in the future? How do we make the judgments that will correctly channel our energies? These decisions call for prayer and action.

All of us must take a careful look at who we are as individuals, congregations, conferences, and as a denomination. We need to review our heritage to understand what has brought us to this point. We must look at our values and sense what it is necessary for us to take into the future. We must look at the future and begin to make conscious decisions about what will be important. What will we see as crucial in relation to the Christian faith? How will we communicate our convictions? How will each individual, congregation, and conference share and be motivated by our values?

The way we move into the future is not a matter of intellectual knowledge, nor is it a matter of developing the right techniques. It really is not a matter of the financial resources we have at our disposal. Our move into the future will be governed essentially by our commitment—its nature and content. John Wesley was trained intellectually and nurtured religiously. He understood the Christian faith as a matter of knowledge and information. But when he understood it as a matter of *intense personal conviction,* he began to change the tenor of the society in which he lived, to influence the lives of countless persons. It was the power of the sense of assurance and the need to communicate this to others that motivated Wesley.

What is our commitment to our faith and to the future? How do we, individually and collectively, understand our task in the name of Christ? It must involve more than just intellectual willingness. It must carry our conviction that the future is a great arena for the realization of God's full potential in each individual life and in society as a whole.

A vital piety must undergird those things we attempt in the name of God. We must proceed with a deep intimate sense that God has acted in our own lives. Yet more, we must be committed to our responsibility to share with others this sense of God's grace. We must join together "in connection" as United Methodists, as the people of the assurance, to combine our prayers, presence, gifts, and service to reach out to others. With a vital piety and clarity of purpose, the founders of our denomination moved into their first century with power to do

God's will as they understood it. So, too, will it be possible for us, with a vital piety and a clear purpose, to move into our third century to transform lives and our nation.

Questions for Consideration

1. What are the primary guides to inform our Christian life and deepen our faith?
2. What does it mean to share our faith and be "in connection" with others as United Methodists?
3. What are the important factors in our own personal Christian experiences? How can we share these with others?
4. What is our commitment to our Christian faith? What must we do to proclaim this faith in Christ?

CHAPTER 4

We Gather Together

Our commitment to Jesus Christ is an individual act. Each of us, at some point, makes a decision to accept Christ as our Savior and to participate in the assurance of the redemption and reconciliation which we receive through the grace of God. However, we cannot live out our commitment to this faith in isolation from one another. As we proclaim, build, and serve, we must work with others who also share in the Christian faith. Our forebears knew that this was an absolute necessity, for they sang, "We gather together to ask the Lord's blessing."

In this chapter we will explore the crucial role of the local congregation, where we gather to strengthen our faith and to go out in witness and service as United Methodists.

The Local Congregation—Our Gathering

The Preamble to the Constitution of The United Methodist Church states that "the Church is a community of all true believers under the Lordship of Christ. It is the redeemed and redeeming fellowship in which the Word of God is preached by persons divinely called, and the Sacraments are duly administered according to Christ's own appointment. Under the discipline of the Holy Spirit, the Church seeks to provide for the maintenance of worship, the edification of believers, and the redemption of the world."[1]

The Preamble clearly states the major roles of the local congregation: to maintain worship, to edify believers, and to redeem the world. Let us explore each of these tasks.

For the Worship of God and the Proclamation of the Faith

Worship is central in the life of the Christian, and it takes on an added dimension in the gathered Community. It is here that the great celebrations and festivals of the Church are shared. Here too the important events in the life of the individual Christian take place: baptism, marriage, confirmation, instruction, fellowship, funeral. The worship life of the local church is extremely important and is characterized by two key elements.

1. *The Proclamation of the Word.* In the Protestant tradition, the congregation gathers to hear the minister proclaim and interpret the message of the Christian faith. The sermon is the primary way this message is communicated. Each person is expected to be actively involved in absorbing the meaning of that which is being presented, since the response to the message must come from the individual, for the proclamation of the message as such has no power unless it is received and acted upon.

The sacraments, while very important in the Protestant tradition, are no longer considered the sole avenue by which to receive and understand God's grace, nor is the Protestant priest or minister the channel through which God's grace is available to the believer. It is the Word itself, the message, that is the vehicle for God's grace—not the minister or sacraments alone. This shift in emphasis is extremely important, for now the reading of the Scriptures and the hearing of the message have become the responsibility of each person. Protestant worship emphasizes proclamation by the preacher and response by the individual and the congregation.

In the early years of United Methodism, preaching focused on the individual in need and on the assurance that God's forgiveness and grace are available to each person. It emphasized God's restoring and redeeming love, and its message of hope called for a response by those who heard. This proclamation of the Word of God took place in churches, fields, groves, houses, barns—wherever there was space to accommodate the listeners.

The proclaiming of the Word also occurred in groups smaller than the total congregation. In societies and classes, prayer fellowships and informal gatherings, individual Christians told of their Christian faith experiences. Lay people witnessed to one another. Here the formal proclamation of the worship services were restated and reinterpreted in personal and intimate terms. Especially in our early history, lay people regularly performed this function. Instruction and guidance of one another in the Christian faith were deemed to be the fundamental tasks of the laity.

In the earliest years of United Methodism, much of the preaching, even in formal worship settings, was done by lay people. This practice continued into the era of the circuit rider, since the ordained minister was frequently absent or at other points on the circuit. Notwithstanding the remarkable ability of our denomination to provide clergy, the responsibility for proclamation and witness was often carried by the laity.

This emphasis on United Methodist lay preachers has diminished through the years. Even their titles have changed. According to the current *Book of Discipline, local pastors,* not *lay preachers,* are certified to serve local churches under some circumstances. We have lay *speakers* (not lay *preachers*) who are trained and certified to preach in the absence of an ordained minister. As a denomination, we no longer license lay people to be "exhorters," formerly an office of some importance, as evidenced by these words published in 1872: "The duties and privileges of an exhorter are to hold meetings for prayer and exhortation whenever an opportunity is afforded, subject to the direction of the preacher in charge. . . . Where there was a scarcity of ministers the exhorter often did important service."[2]

The task of proclaiming the faith should not be left solely to the clergy, though time and custom have developed a tendency for the laity to assume that it is the prerogative of the minister alone. Some pastors have failed to encourage lay people to witness to their beliefs (some even have actively discouraged them). Proclaiming the faith is a commission that is given to every Christian. We ignore this commission at our peril.

This is not an attempt to diminish the role of the ordained minister. The preacher has always been central in the proclamation of the Word. Indeed, the United Brethren, Evangelical, and Methodist conferences all began as associations of ministers who were seeking the best way to utilize their clergy and their other available resources. United Methodism did not begin as an association of congregations wishing to develop a larger organization. Nor did we begin as a group of persons dedicated to a particular doctrinal formulation or affirmation. The annual conference, as the primary unit, developed from efforts to provide for the licensing and ordaining of clergy, the establishment of areas to be served, and the orderly appointment and supervision of ministers. In large measure, this remains one of its most important tasks.

There has been renewed interest in liturgy and celebration of the sacraments in recent years, but the preaching of the Word continues to be the foremost component of worship for the gathered community of faith. United Methodists continue to affirm the need for the message of God to be proclaimed and interpreted to the congregation.

We believe that the ordination of ministers specifically sets them aside to provide the scholarship and interpretation necessary to make God's message relevant for the congregation. This is their key function, more important than the organizational life of the congregation, more important than the district and annual conference organizational needs, and more important than many community activities.

Christians gather together in order to be that "redeemed and redeeming fellowship in which the Word of God is preached." They gather, as well, to understand more fully the nature of the call to witness and to serve. The practice of witness and service will not take the same form for every person, but each Christian's response to God's grace is not complete until he or she shares intimately and directly in proclaiming the faith. It is not sufficient to hear and receive only; one also must share.

2. *The Sacraments.* As United Methodists, we proclaim our faith also through the observance of two sacraments, the Lord's Supper (Holy Communion) and the sacrament of baptism. These sacraments, which we share with most Protestant denominations, remind each of us, in the context of the total congregation, of our significant relationship with God.

In the baptism of youth and adults, each person declares that he or she has repented and accepted Jesus Christ as Savior. Each affirms a belief in God and the desire to follow God's commandments. Upon this profession of faith, each is then baptized. In the baptism of children, the parents confess their faith in Christ and accept the responsibility to live in accordance with and to instruct their child in the Christian faith.

In contrast with some Christian bodies, United Methodists usually celebrate the sacrament of baptism as a part of congregational worship. The gathered congregation reaffirms its faith and assumes responsibility for supporting and nurturing the faith of the person being baptized. Thus a baptism is more than a solitary act for one person and his or her immediate family; it is a sacrament that involves the entire worshiping community. It is a time for the total congregation to again proclaim its faith, and also to witness, through its pledge to undergird the new member in the Christian community.

In like manner, the sacrament of Holy Communion is a time for the total congregation to reaffirm its faith. As part of the celebration, those in the congregation, both individually and collectively, ask for the forgiveness of sins and receive again the assurance of God's love and grace made possible through Jesus Christ. Partaking of the Lord's Supper, we remember the promise of God to each of us individually, and we also jointly share and commemorate Christ's act of redemption. It becomes a collective action through which the Community reaffirms and testifies to its commitment to God.

In both these sacraments, we celebrate the assurance that grace belongs to each of us when we come to God in sincere repentance. Each person's relationship with God is reaffirmed. The sacraments provide the opportunity to profess our commitment in the context of the total community and to share with one another in remembrance, in reaffirmation, and in proclamation.

Worship in the Congregation. Worship is the most important activity of the gathered congregation. Through the various services and settings, members of the congregation begin to appreciate who they are, individually and collectively, in relation to God and to one another. For those who share their faith and participate in worship, the experience serves several functions. Four are discussed here.

1. Worship affirms and confirms the individual in relation-ship with God. We approach God with reverence and awe, and

we respond with praise, thanksgiving, and dedication. In worship with others, we testify to our faith by our very presence.

2. Worship brings the congregation together most frequently. It provides a setting for the total Community to share in the collective prayers, affirmations, and hymns of the church. We have the opportunity to be with others who may need our guidance and support, and from whom we can obtain support for ourselves.

3. Worship helps to clarify our identity and purpose as Christians. It enables us to hear the proclamation of the Word and to respond to our great commission to share this message with others.

4. Worship provides motivation for our active response to God. Through worship, we are informed of our responsibility to develop our Christian life and share it through witness and service.

Our relationship with God deepens, and the life of the congregation is strengthened when we participate in meaningful worship experiences. "A revitalization of worship with a recovery of the power of the liturgical life of the church, and with baptism and holy communion brought back to the center along with biblical and pastoral preaching, will speak to the search for mystery, transcendence, and personal experience of grace."[3] Worship is the way God's message is proclaimed and affirmed, the way we dedicate our lives and discover our active role of service to others.

For Prayer, Study, and Discipline in the Building of the Church

The Christian needs the community of faith not only for worship, but for study and nurture. It is clear that Wesley never envisioned the Christian in isolation.

Wesley believed that small groups were the key to Christian life. Unsatisfied with what he perceived to be the lack of community in the Church of England, Wesley insisted that the Methodist people be members of small groups. He established band societies and classes in which the people learned, shared, prayed, and reexamined their Christian practices. The development of these groups and the constant nurturing of them by Methodist leaders was the fundamental aspect of Wesley's program.[4]

The importance of such groups in the life of a congregation cannot be overestimated. The vitality of a congregation depends on the quality of ministerial leadership, but also on the strength and character of its various groups. Indeed, the latter may be even more important. For it is in small groups that the Community ministers to itself, sharing its faith in nurture and service.

Christians have two primary tasks—as individuals and as members of congregations. Let us briefly examine each.

1. A primary obligation of the Christian is *to grow in the faith*. We have discussed the importance of the individual's response to God. Such growth is encouraged by the knowledge that we can "move on toward perfection" in love in our relationship with God. This becomes part of the obligation of the gathered community as well, whether in terms of total congregation, classes, or small groups. In every setting, each person is to be aided in the development of a deeper and more mature Christian faith. As we grow in our understanding of the gifts we receive as Christians and of the responsibilities we have assumed, we are to sustain and direct one another. The congregation must provide a setting in which members can give mutual guidance and support.

2. The second major responsibility of the Christian is *to develop the disciplines* that make growth and witness possible. Committed Christians are to engage in activities that will inform and guide their living in response to God. In our faith community we are to help and encourage one another to develop such disciplines, four of which are suggested here; there may well be others. These should be considered in terms of what each of us should undertake for our own spiritual development, and also in terms of how we can assist one another within the congregation.

a. *Bible Study.* It may seem unnecessary to mention Bible study, yet many Christians—many United Methodists—do not engage in any systematic reading and study of the Bible, the beginning point for understanding God's revelations to us.

This is not to be a solitary discipline. While we are to study for our own enlightenment, we are also to encourage one another to know more of the Bible, to comprehend and appreciate its message, and to search for its meaning in today's world. Many resources have been developed by those within the denomination who are concerned that we learn more about God's Word. The Scriptures come alive as we read, share, and discuss them. This is a discipline that we must develop in ourselves and encourage in others.

b. *Prayer.* As our faith matures we become aware of the necessity and power of prayer; it should be experienced as a living and vital force in our lives. While prayer is a very personal discipline, it can be encouraged and enhanced by sharing it with others. A disciplined prayer life can be a powerful factor in the growth and development of faith and commitment, both for individuals and for congregations. One of the obligations we mutually assume as Christians is the development and sharing of our prayer life.

c. *Christian Living.* We must develop the determination to live our lives in accordance with God's commandments, not an easy task in today's world. As the ethical and moral standards of society change, many different perspectives are presented to us. Each of us must make key decisions in light of our Christian faith, and both Bible study and prayer help to inform those choices.

In order to live according to Christian standards, however, we need the support of a Christian community. *Many of us struggle to live a Christian life in the absence of a sound knowledge of biblical teachings, with a poorly developed prayer life, and with little interaction with other members of our congregation.* We can benefit from frequent interaction with other Christians in establishing moral principles to govern our lives. We should provide one another with mutual encouragement to develop these values in our relationships with others and with God.

d. *Service.* As we develop the disciplines of Bible study, prayer, and Christian living, we will understand not only the meaning of God's will for our lives, but how we are to respond. The discipline of active outreach and service is extremely important and should be seen in the context of the total community of faith. We need mutual support and encouragement from others to clarify our opportunities, to assess our skills and resources, and to ascertain ways to respond.

Perhaps this may not seem to be a separate discipline, but we cannot receive the power of the message of reconciliation without also discovering ways to respond. In community with others, we must find opportunities for outreach and service.

Throughout our history, lay United Methodists have been important in providing growth and nurture for one another in congregations and classes. Lay people have carried the major responsibility for explaining the meaning of the Scriptures and for urging (or exhorting) fellow Christians to grow in the disciplined life of study, prayer, ethical living, and service. They have assumed responsibility for the building up of the Church, and they have cared for one another's needs.

While United Methodists today still show considerable concern for one another, we find less emphasis on the four disciplines noted above. We evidence our concern especially in times of life crises—major illness, sudden tragedy, death. Yet we are hesitant, even when we are together in church-related classes and groups, to inquire about one another's spiritual concerns, problems, and needs.

Lay ministries have been and remain extremely important. Indeed, when responding to the vows of baptism and reception into membership, United Methodists pledge that they will take responsibility for the nurture of new members of the fellowship. Because the words of these vows reaffirm the great responsibility given to each Christian, they are not to be taken lightly.

For Service and Action

By hearing the faith proclaimed, by participating in worship, and by developing disciplines for growth, we discover how we can best respond to God's action in our lives.

But in recent years, our sense of purpose has been blurred by the contrasting and competing claims of many activities and programs. United Methodists struggle to comprehend and deal with the multitude of requests for service. Our difficulty is twofold—we are not able to sort out effectively all the emphases placed before us, and we are not completely sure what our main focus as individuals and congregations should be.

Service and action must flow from our personal experience in the faith and our collective reflection as a Christian community. *If as individuals we are uncertain about our faith commitment, we cannot be readily motivated to fulfill a call for service.* If as congregations we are uncertain about our faith commitment, we cannot act collectively with conviction and power.

If we receive a personal assurance of God's grace, study and discipline ourselves in that assurance, and then do not respond in witness and action, we leave an essential element of the Christian faith unfulfilled. Many congregations, in exploring the Christian life together, do not adequately examine their reasons for witness and outreach. All of us are called to be in mission to others. "There is no Christian theology apart from a missionary theology. There is no person called Christian who may avoid participating in outreach."[5]

Random action, either by individuals or by congregations, fails to fulfill the requirements of the Christian faith. We cannot act apart from one another or capriciously. A well-conceived, concerted witness is needed. Nor can we act solely on the basis of custom or tradition. When we are bound by our personal or collective pasts to the extent that we cannot explore new concepts or new calls for service, our action is unduly constricted. While we can give grateful thanks for the significant work that already has been done in the name of Christ by United Methodists, we cannot blindly accept all that has been completed, instituted, or is currently in process.

Do our traditions and past actions provide appropriate opportunities for witness and service today and in the future? To the extent that they still commend themselves, we should rededicate our efforts to their successful continuance and completion. To the degree that they are no longer appropriate or fruitful, we should be willing to redirect, modify, or discontinue them. Service that is not appropriate, productive, or enabling will not ultimately fulfill the needs of either the church or the individuals.

Part of our task is to discover the purpose and motivation for our response to God. Service and witness issue forth most effectively from our mature understandings of ourselves in the faith. This comes about in three ways. First, our reasons for response are clarified as we understand the requirements of the Christian faith. Just as individuals must realize the need to act, congregations, too, must realize that need. Yet we must first learn who we are as a people of God and how we can best respond.

Second, clarity of purpose enables us to channel our efforts most appropriately: When we can see clearly the type of witness that is needed, we can prepare ourselves for an appropriate response.

Third, as we understand our purpose as a people of God, we find the motivation to act—to devote our presence, prayers, gifts, and service to clearly perceived goals. We can act with understanding. Our worship and study are not then seen in isolation, but as important means of preparing ourselves and becoming motivated for witness and service. Without that motivation, sufficient commitment to accomplish the tasks is not attained.

Robert L. Wilson describes a congregation coming to understand itself in the Christian faith.

> A congregation must love itself before it is capable of loving others. A congregation will not love its neighbors in a vibrant, committed way until it has first learned to love its own witness, its own tradition, its own message, its own life together. A congregation must first be confident and optimistic about itself before it will be motivated to share itself with the world. In fact, before it experiences the gospel within its own congregational life, a congregation more than likely has no gospel to share with anyone else.[6]

So we gather as Christians. The congregation's power for worship, nurture, and witness exceeds the sum of the individuals who comprise it. The congregation has the potential to be a vital, significant instrument of Christian power and love; yet the full strength of this collective force is rarely exercised. We are challenged to explore and examine the life and character of the congregation. Lack of collective vision causes many congregations to focus on their own survival and institutional needs, rather than on the greater commitment to service in God's name. As it is possible for an individual, so too it is possible for a congregation, as the gathered community of believers, to be actively and effectively involved in proclamation of the faith, building up the Church, and service to the world.

The Local Congregation—Our Going Forth

We gather together in the unique fellowship of the Christian community—in congregations, classes, and fellowship groups. We gather for worship, study and nurture, friendship, and service within the congregation. So gathered, we have a responsibility to discover ways to reach out beyond the lives, beyond the boundaries of the congregation.

For Proclamation and Witness

A primary responsibility of the congregation is to proclaim the message of God in Christ. This responsibility cannot be ignored. The message is proclaimed in worship and preaching, and also in witness and service. The congregation can fulfill this responsibility in three ways.

1. *Preparation.* The congregation must prepare itself individually and collectively to proclaim the assurance of God's love and forgiveness. We discussed this extremely important task at some length in the preceding section. It may appear that the worship, sacraments, study, and nurture shared within the congregation are only for the benefit of the members' spiritual growth. However, these same activities also help to prepare Christians to proclaim and live out their convictions with others.

Upon close examination, those congregations that decline and/or die share a common trait. Their plight generally has not resulted from inadequate resources, wrong location, poor ministerial leadership, or competition from other churches, but from the *lack of a sense of mission,* the consequence of superficial or inadequate conviction, motivation, and preparation! The congregation has seen its task as the protecting of what is or what has been, rather than the proclaiming of God's message through witness and outreach.

Without preparation, we do not possess the spiritual depth of vision to appreciate what God has done and is doing through us. We are most effective when we are confirmed and strengthened in our faith through knowledge, prayer, and discussion about the content of our faith. Preparation both reveals the call to service and supports us in answering that call.

2. *Participation.* The congregation must directly involve itself in proclaiming the faith. This requires active participation in the quest for those who need God's saving love: Members must be willing to strive to increase the faith-commitment of marginally active and inactive members, willing to search for those not related to the congregation and the Christian Church. Preparation of each member and of the entire congregation through worship, study, and prayer will undergird sincere, purposeful outreach.

All members will not be called upon to perform the same types of tasks. But in every endeavor, the congregation as a whole will be supported by all the members through their presence, prayers, gifts, and service. In some cases participation will mean meeting immediate human needs of others in the immediate area. Care of the poor, the homeless, the distressed, the lonely, or the aged is an example of service and witness that can be actively carried out in the name of Christ.

It is most important that active proclamation and service be accomplished not merely by the minister or other professionally employed leadership. Active response to God is the responsibility of all the members, and their willingness to commit themselves will be reflected in the total life of the congregation. If the majority of the members are passive, so will be the outlook and stance of the congregation. The pastor can guide and lead, but cannot and should not carry the whole load.

Those within and outside the community of believers must know that the congregation is a group of Christians gathered together to serve. If the whole congregation actively shares in this response to God's love, then all will know that it is indeed an active, vital, and relevant part of the Body of Christ.

3. *Proxy.* It is not possible for all of us to be directly involved in the many activities of the Christian Church throughout the world. We choose to be part of a United Methodist congregation—partly because of our perception of what the local congregation does, and partly because of our understanding of what the whole denomination represents and is accomplishing.

We support proclamation and service beyond the local

church by proxy: We authorize others to serve on our behalf. We choose to support their endeavors by actions taken in our local church meetings and through decisions of our delegates to annual and general conferences. Because we are "in connection" with one another, we share in the decisions and obligations to support those endeavors. *Part of our being "in connection" with others allows us to provide proclamation and service that we could not provide individually, or even through our local church.*

The church is at work in the annual conference and throughout the nation and world. We are there by spirit and intent—we are there by proxy. We support the work of evangelism, mission, and education, showing our concern by our prayers, our gifts, and our active interest. Each individual is involved in that proclamation and service as a part of the total Christian commitment to serve in God's name, and also as a part of the congregation's support of those activities.

We are not often made aware of this connection, but those in service throughout the world need our thoughts and prayers. The prayer calendar developed by the Women's Division of the General Board of Global Ministries helps to keep distant needs in our thoughts and prayers.

As our own faith is nurtured and strengthened, so will be our motivation and commitment to support, by proxy, Christians everywhere in the world who are proclaiming and serving in God's name.

For All Who Will Receive Christ

A major part of our task as Christians, as United Methodists, is to proclaim the faith. The logical question, then, is, To whom shall we go? The answer is that *we are to go to everyone who will listen to us.* That is the great commission given by Christ: "Go therefore and make disciples of all nations, baptizing them in the name of the Father and of the Son and of the Holy Spirit, teaching them to observe all that I have commanded you" (Matt. 28:19-20 RSV).

To whom shall we go? In a real sense, this is an irrelevant question. We are called to share our Christian witness and God's love with all who have not yet heard it or who have not yet been willing to accept it. Ultimately, we may not ask the question. We must simply go to any and all who are in need of God's saving grace.

At first this seems to be a quite obvious truth. Yet as individuals and as congregations, we have not always acted on the basis of such an obvious and apparent truth. We tend to draw subtle distinctions and establish artificial boundaries which we are unwilling or unable to cross when proclaiming our faith or sharing in Christian fellowship. Why do individuals and congregations become self-limiting? One reason is that we have insufficient grounding in the meaning and content of our faith. Another reason is that we fail to devote sufficient time and energy to developing the personal and corporate disciplines required of Christians. As a consequence, congregations, and sometimes even the entire denomination only partially or inadequately answer that question—To whom shall we go?

We tend to seek first those with whom we are comfortable, those whom we know, those who are like us. We feel that if we can work with those persons first, the time will come to seek out others. That may be a beginning. But if we stop there, we participate in a subtle form of heresy and a not-so-subtle form of self-deception.

Where does one draw the boundaries for proclaiming God's message? We cannot sort out persons on the basis of their personal history, age, sex, racial or ethnic background, economic status, political perspective, theological stance, or any other factor. Our task is proclaiming and being willing to share Christian fellowship with any who will respond. Some will respond, receive Christ, and be willing to join with us. Some will receive Christ and prefer to become part of another Christian group. Some will turn both from Christ and from us. But we must always remember that the choice is theirs. It is not our prerogative to choose who shall hear and receive. Our task is to proclaim and to share with anyone who will listen.

Our strength as United Methodists is not in our pluralism or diversity, however important that may be. *Our strength results from our willingness to proclaim God's truth to all persons and to welcome all who respond.* Our strength comes as we welcome into communion with us all who will join with us, regardless of their past or their present. Our strength comes as we join together wholeheartedly and unreservedly in Christ's name, to move into the future as a truly United Methodism. To paraphrase Matthew 6:31-33: Therefore, do not be anxious, saying, "To whom shall we go?" but seek first God's kingdom and all these shall be yours as well.

Service to the World

How are we to be in service in the world and who is to be involved?

We discover opportunities for service as we develop our individual and corporate commitment to Christ. Our commitment is the foundation upon which we build our faith-experience and the point from which we move to be of service. If that commitment is shallow or faulty, our service will be shallow and faulty as well.

We strengthen our commitment through prayerful examination of our own relationship to God in faith and through the study and nurture of our Christian experience. We do this both as individuals and in our collective worship, mutual support, and guidance. With a strong commitment born of personal experience, knowledge of the Scriptures, and prayerful examination of our faith, we are prepared to seek ways to respond to God in service and love.

We are called to be actively involved. The ways we respond may differ, but there must be a response. Congregations, as well as individuals, are called to be in mission and service. A faith commitment turned only inward will soon wither; our Christian faith requires us to share it with others.

As Christians, we have accepted the responsibility to participate directly in witness and outreach. As members of The United Methodist Church, we have committed ourselves to support our denomination, and through it the Body of Christ Universal, with our presence, prayers, gifts, and service. We discover ways to do this within our congregation and community. We can take direct action to extend the Christian faith to those in spiritual or physical need.

We also serve indirectly by supporting others in their witness and outreach. Through our active interest, prayers, and gifts, we extend the ministry of our church beyond the geography of our own parish. We are able to reach, in the name of Christ, people we will never see. We do this through devoted Christians we may never meet. We respond not from duty, not grudgingly or hesitantly, but with a sense of confidence and joy in those who act on our behalf. It is our conviction that this is a part of God's work.

As individual Christians, we join together to celebrate what God in Christ has done for us. As a congregation, we seek to understand the meaning of God's action. By seeking, we discover our purpose and motivation to respond. The priorities are the same for the congregation as for the individual—to proclaim the faith, build the Church, and serve the world.

Questions for Consideration

1. What are the three major functions or activities that should take place in our local congregation?
2. How well are these functions performed in our congregation?
3. How is each local church to fulfill its task of active proclamation and witness?
4. Why are there to be no boundaries or limitations placed on our proclamation of God's message?

CHAPTER 5

To Spread Scriptural Holiness

After the time of its organization in 1784, United Methodism moved with vigor across the United States as the new nation developed. In the earliest days, there was little to predict the success of the Methodist, United Brethren, or Evangelical groups. They had limited financial resources; for the most part, their few congregations were poorly housed or met in borrowed quarters; their preachers were usually young, inexperienced, and poorly trained; they could provide few books for their preachers and members. Their organizations were as new as the nation, struggling to develop their character while they accomplished their tasks.

There was little to recommend those groups to the future, except for one fundamental quality. The movements had a vision, a purpose, and a commitment to devote their all to accomplish that purpose. The first *Discipline* of the Methodist Episcopal Church, written in 1785 in the form of questions and answers, contains the statement that focused and marshaled the energies of the new denomination.

Q. What may we reasonably believe to be God's Design in raising up the Preachers called *Methodists*?
A. To reform the Continent, and to spread scriptural Holiness over these Lands.[1]

The United Brethren in Christ and the Evangelical Association subsequently incorporated similar statements into their *Disciplines*.

In this chapter and the next, we will consider, in reverse order, the two parts of this answer and their importance and relevance for us today.

93

The Call to Spread Scriptural Holiness over These Lands

The movements which developed into United Methodism had a purpose: to proclaim the Word of God to as many persons as possible, both inside and outside the Church—and all those "in connection" with the new churches were involved. This purpose was widely understood and agreed upon, and actively pursued by lay people and ministers alike. There was not always complete agreement as to the methods or the organization needed to support the task, but the underlying purpose was clear and served as a significant criterion for deciding how resources and personnel were to be utilized. Let us explore some elements of this call and the necessary responses.

Our Understanding of the Zeal to Spread Scriptural Holiness

"Scriptural Holiness" is the concept (discussed earlier) used by Wesley to emphasize the power of God's forgiveness and reconciliation in our lives. We are assured of this through Jesus Christ, and we receive it by our response, our faith in him as Savior. As forgiven committed Christians, we are given the opportunity to move toward that perfection in love to be found in relationship with God, a relationship that includes other persons and society. Thus we can grow into holiness, according to our understanding of God's acts as revealed in the Scriptures.

These are powerful concepts. They speak to each of us. They do not require special skills or knowledge—only the faith and full commitment of the individual. They speak to each person's fulfillment in relationship to God, in this life and in the next. Each of us can know that we are now new creatures in God—that is the power of this statement of faith. Wesley provided a renewed understanding of God's love for all people. The individual's faith response benefits from, but is not dependent on the sacraments, the pronouncements of the organized church, the mediation of the clergy, or a stated and prescribed catechism. It depends on the individual who hears, receives, and acts on this renewed understanding of scriptural holiness. There was power in Wesley's emphasis, and there is power in each person who comes into a restored relationship with God.

One's understanding of God's effect on one's life is

accompanied by a commitment to action. If God acted for us, God will act also for every other person who responds in faith. Because this is true, each Christian has the obligation to make this message of scriptural holiness available to as many others as possible. And this became the driving force behind the goal "to spread scriptural Holiness over these Lands." How could one receive God's love, understanding what it had done in one's own life, and not desire to share this with others? The conviction of God's loving action in each person's life, coupled with its availability to all others through faith, provided the zeal to proclaim the Word.

But proclamation is not a solitary act. As the individual shares his or her faith by coming "in connection" with other Christians, spreading the message becomes a collective venture. From its inception, the strength of United Methodism has lain in the fact that its organizational structure was not developed to serve only those already within the faith community. It developed to provide adequate means for witness and service. The current decline in United Methodist membership may well be correlated with the denomination's increasing preoccupation with its own institutional and organizational concerns. It also may be correlated with our emphasis on secular social action rather than on the proclamation of the message of God.

The annual conference was established to provide a scattered and growing constituency with preaching and celebration of the sacraments, and to facilitate the spreading of the message of scriptural holiness as Methodists, Evangelicals, and United Brethren understood it.

We should reflect seriously on the motivations that hold our congregations and annual conferences together today. What great principles govern our deliberations and actions? Most of us either cannot say or can offer only a broad generalization, barren of zeal or commitment. The early Methodist movement was unified partially by its sense of identity and purpose. Methodists, as well as their United Brethren and Evangelical counterparts, were people of the assurance, committed to sharing their message of scriptural holiness to all who would hear and receive.

Is the task complete? Are we now at the point in history where we can concentrate primarily on perfecting our institutions and organization in order to consolidate our Christian expression of faith? The answer is clearly *No.* Much remains to be done!

We have discussed the continuing need for each Christian to practice the basic disciplines of spiritual life so that growth in the faith will continue. Congregations, too, should practice similar disciplines to prepare their members to nurture one another and to enable them to focus more effectively on the witness and outreach required of them. Annual conferences, as well as the total denomination, also need to practice these disciplines.

The call remains: Spread scriptural holiness, proclaim the faith. We prepare ourselves to do this through understanding our faith, through growing in the spiritual disciplines, and through exploring the requirements of witness and service that must be carried out in God's name. At our peril, do we become preoccupied with ourselves. We fail if we become merely preservers of our past and our resources, for we are called to share. We fail if we focus only on those now within our community of faith, for we are called to witness. We fail if we address only our own spiritual and human needs, for we are called to serve.

To paraphrase the question asked at the Christmas Conference of 1784, What may we reasonably believe to have been God's design in raising up a people called United Methodists? What is our answer? The enormous zeal that has driven the United Methodist movement for most of its two hundred years has focused on proclaiming the faith. In recent decades, however, the forward thrust of the denomination has waned. Do we need a new statement in response to the key question? A restatement of the initial response? A resurgence of commitment and zeal? A spiritual revival? Our commission from God has not changed—we are to spread scriptural holiness and proclaim the faith.

Witness and Service—The Ministry of All Christians

Who among us is to spread scriptural holiness? Where does responsibility lie?

There are some clear guidelines for answering these questions. As a denomination, we are guided and regulated by the legislative enactments of the General Conference. The contents of *The Book of Discipline* represents the current thinking and action of the denomination. While we read *The Discipline* for guidance in administrative and organizational aspects of our life "in connection" with one another, we also find there some extraordinarily important passages to guide our reflections about our purpose as United Methodists. One section deals with the nature of ministry.

> All Christian ministry is Christ's ministry of outreaching love. The Christian Church, as the Body of Christ, is that community whose members share both his mind and mission. The heart of Christian ministry is shown by a common life of gratitude and devotion, witness and service, celebration, and discipleship. All Christians are called to this ministry of servanthood in the world to the glory of God and for human fulfillment. The forms of this ministry are diverse in locale, in interest, and in denominational accent, yet also always catholic in spirit and outreach (¶ 101).[2]

Further, we are informed that we are all part of this ministry as the normal, consistent, and required response to God's redeeming love. Again, the action of the 1980 General Conference informs us:

> This general ministry of all Christians in Christ's name and spirit is both a gift and a task. The gift is God's unmerited grace; the task is unstinting service. Entrance into the Church is acknowledged in Baptism and may include persons of all ages. In this Sacrament the Church claims God's promise, "the seal of the Spirit" (Ephesians 1:13). Baptism is followed by nurture and the consequent awareness by the baptized of the claim to ministry in Christ placed upon their lives by the Church. Such a ministry is ratified in confirmation, where the pledges of Baptism are accepted and renewed for life and mission. Entrance into and acceptance of ministry begin in a local church, but the impulse to minister always moves one beyond the congregation toward the whole human community (¶ 105).[3]

This is the ministry into which all of us move upon our acceptance of God's grace and our membership in the Christian community. We have tended, in recent years, to define the concepts of ministry rather narrowly—preaching, and the calling and nurturing of members. Many clergy accept sole responsibility for those tasks, delegated to them by lay people who feel that they themselves are accomplishing their proper role by helping to provide compensation for the pastor and housing of the congregation.

Yet *all* of us are required by our faith commitment to participate in the tasks of witness and service in God's name! It is not a responsibility reserved to ordained ministers, employed staff persons, or elected lay leaders of local congregations and annual conferences. It is an obligation that is placed on *every* Christian, every United Methodist! In recent years we have not explored the full ramifications of this mandate. As we have made our organization and ministry increasingly more formal and professional, many lay people have sensed that it is no longer appropriate for them to be actively involved in direct witness and service. It is a serious mistake to move in this direction, for an individual or for an organization. Consider this additional word of guidance adopted by the 1980 General Conference.

> The people of God are the Church made visible in the world. It is they who must convince the world of the reality of the gospel or leave it unconvinced. There can be no evasion or delegation of this responsibility; the Church is either faithful as a witnessing and serving community, or it loses its vitality and its impact on an unbelieving world (¶ 106).[4]

Unintentionally, the General Conference may well have described the source of distress and decline within The United Methodist Church today. As a people of God, we may not be convincing the world of the reality of the gospel. Are we evading our responsibility, or seeking to delegate it to others? If we are not completely faithful as a witnessing and serving community, then we become increasingly irrelevant, for we are devoting our interests and strengths to other than our primary task.

It is extraordinarily important that the total membership of our denomination regain its zeal for witnessing and outreach. We must clearly understand what this means and discover how we can be actively engaged in the task. Perhaps we will need to study Wesley's emphases for understanding our Christian faith. Perhaps we must seriously reconsider our primary purpose as a people of God. In any case, lay people must become motivated to rediscover their significant role in witnessing to God's redeeming love, wherever there is need to hear God's message and wherever there is human need.

The commission to spread scriptural holiness over the land was actively carried out by lay people in the early years of our church. There is no question but that The United Methodist Church must place a renewed emphasis on *general* ministry—the witnessing and serving of all Christians, to seek out and nurture all who are in need of the saving message of Christ.

Word, Sacrament, and Order—The Ordained Ministry

Within the United Methodist tradition, we have always had those who were chosen by the church for a specific function—what is termed the *representative* ministry. These people have felt an inner call to devote themselves fully to the work of God. In light of their training and personal character, and upon due examination by the church, they are set aside to serve in special roles of responsibility. There are also diaconal ministers—lay people consecrated by their annual conferences to devote themselves to specialized and distinctive ministry. I will focus on those in the representative ministry who are ordained by the church to be in full-time ministry on behalf of the total church, as described excellently in *The Book of Discipline.*

The ordained ministers are called to specialized ministries of Word, Sacrament, and Order. Through these distinctive functions ordained ministers devote themselves wholly to the work of the Church and to the upbuilding of the general ministry. They do this through careful study of the Scripture and its faithful interpretation, through effective proclamation of the gospel and responsible administration of the Sacraments, through diligent pastoral leadership of their congregations for fruitful discipleship, and by following the guidance of the Holy Spirit in witnessing beyond the congregation in the local community and to the ends of the earth. The ordained ministry is defined by its intentionally representative character, by its passion for the hallowing of life, and by its concern to link all local ministries with the widest boundaries of the Christian community (¶ 109).[5]

There are two key phrases in this paragraph. The first is that which refers to the "intentionally representative character" of ordained ministers. These people are not to replace the laity. They *represent* the total membership in many activities. They are to provide guidance in the celebration of the sacraments on behalf of the Community. Through their study and interpretation of the Scripture, they are to facilitate the congregation in its understanding of the Christian faith. The ordained minister does not replace the general ministers, but devotes his or her special skills to providing guidance for the life and work of the congregation.

The second important phrase tells us that the ordained ministers are to devote themselves to "the upbuilding of the general ministry." They are to use their skills and training to strengthen and nurture the congregation, to the end that its members can perform their tasks of witness and service. Ordained ministers have three specific tasks.

1. *Word.* Ordained ministers are expected to be skilled in the content and interpretation of the Scriptures. First, they are to preach, to proclaim the faith both to those within the community of faith and to those still in need of hearing the Word. Second, they are to assist lay members in understanding the faith so that they can be more effective in their crucial witness and service.

2. *Sacrament.* The sacraments are singularly significant acts of worship in our Christian lives together. It is important that those who participate in these sacraments be instructed in their meaning for each person and for the whole congregation. It is a concern of the whole church that the sacraments be administered with reverence, order, and care. The role of the ordained clergy is to provide leadership in administering the sacraments

and in other key services of worship, to help the congregation develop a deeper and richer faith.

3. *Order.* The ordained minister is to guide the organizational aspects of the congregation so that the talents and energies of all are best utilized to meet members' needs and to provide outreach and service. It is their role to help lay people combine their energies, prayers, and resources so that they can achieve the most effective witness and service.

As in the case of the laity, clergy too must recommit themselves to their fundamental tasks. In conjunction with a renewed understanding of the laity's role, the special tasks delegated to ordained ministers must be reexamined.

In recent years ordained ministers have been devoting so much time and attention to the tasks of the *general* ministry that they have had insufficient time for the specialized tasks of the *representative* ministry. Witness and service have been carried out more and more through the efforts of ordained ministers. Furthermore, organizational and structural requirements of the local church and the annual conference (the requirements of "Order") have taken considerable time that the clergy could otherwise have devoted to the upbuilding of laity in mission.

We are called to be ministers in God's church. The task of proclaiming the message of Christ is one which requires the attention of *all* of us. As lay persons or as ordained ministers, we have different ways in which we respond to God's love. What we must understand is that *each* of us is under obligation to respond by sharing our faith. Responsibility for the ministry of witness and service clearly belongs to all of us. Each of us can find a different avenue through which to express our faith and respond. Each of us is to recognize our own unique gifts and be willing to share those gifts. We also are to provide encouragement and support to others who are seeking to serve.

The zeal needed to once again spread scriptural holiness over these lands will be regained when lay people have a new and enlarged vision of what they can and should be doing in and through their Christian faith. The zeal will be regained when ordained ministers focus once again on their special tasks, thereby strengthening lay people for ministry.

Leadership for the Resurgence of the Zeal to Proclaim

Much of the strength and power of the early Methodist movement was focused in its leadership. It was guided by Thomas Coke, Francis Asbury, and the absent but powerful John Wesley. Leadership was crucial for the Evangelicals and the United Brethren as well. The early leaders focused and directed the energies of ministers and lay people alike. These persons led because of the formal authority given to them, but they were leaders primarily because of their inner conviction of the message they proclaimed and their willingness to spend and be spent in the task. Their mission was to spread scriptural holiness, and they were determined to provide the guidance and marshal the resources to accomplish that goal. In our denomination today, we need to examine the role of leadership in asserting the power and zeal to proclaim God's message.

The Call for Leadership and Direction

Great leaders generally share three characteristics: (1) They have a clear understanding of the task to be accomplished; (2) they have an uncompromising determination to devote all available energies to complete that task or mission; and (3) they are willing to involve as many people as possible to see that the work is accomplished. We can observe these characteristics in many of the great leaders of our denomination. Because they are able to focus on the singularity of the task before them, they have been able to accomplish much and to inspire others to accomplish much.

It is easy to idealize and romanticize about the past and to call up visions of the great personalities who guided our denomination's destiny in both its successes and its failures. It is also easy to join in the chorus, asking where all the leaders have gone. Although leadership in general is not held in high esteem today, nevertheless the question of leadership *must* be resolved by any group of persons joined together to accomplish a common task.

United Methodism has moved through its history with significant leadership. We can point to great bishops, great preachers in influential pulpits, and lay leaders who established significant programs of service and outreach. The work of these persons originated with the overall purpose of spreading God's saving word to those who had not embraced it.

United Methodism moved into the 1960s at the peak of its membership, resources, and strength. Countless activities, organizations, and institutions were under our auspices, and we were succeeding in most of what we attempted to do. During that prosperity, two factors began to emerge. First, in the midst of our complex organizational life, we became unable to state with clarity our central purpose or who we perceived ourselves to be. Second, we became unable to reach a consensus as to our appropriate role and mission in relation to the major forces for social change that were emerging in society. Simultaneously, we failed to find leadership able to enlist a broad spectrum of support. Without key leadership to focus and channel our energies, we increasingly found ourselves adrift. Not only did we drift on the denominational level, but in the annual conferences and local churches as well.

Conditions have changed, producing new factors to which we must adapt. Many persons in positions of responsibility have been struggling to treat current situations with perspectives of the past. Many others, who have attempted to provide appropriate responses to the new forces, have not received sufficient support from their constituencies to sustain their leadership. Robert Greenleaf suggests that our idea of what is desirable has changed. "One circumstance that brings on a crisis of institutional quality is that . . . we have suddenly shifted our standard of what is *good*. Whereas, up to recently, *good* was a rank order performance at or near the top of the field, now *good* has become doing what is reasonable and possible with available resources."[6]

Is it possible that we have allowed the definition of a good leader to become "one who is competent at doing what is reasonable with the resources that are available"? Is this what we want in our local churches, annual conferences, denomination? Perhaps we want leaders who can administer the present. Is it possible that as a denomination, we are in fact getting the kind of institutionally oriented leadership we want? Have we utilized some leadership positions as symbolic gestures of our inclusiveness? Are we making gestures, rather than seeking strong leadership? Are we, therefore, not seeking or genuinely not willing to accept those who are able to provide strong leadership in commitment?

What we need today and for the future is leadership with vision, to spur us on in our primary task of spreading scriptural holiness, to remind us of the importance of our response to God's grace, and to help us relate our personal faith to the contemporary world.

Even as we work in many places and in many ways, we must be convinced that our efforts count toward accomplishing our primary tasks as Christians. We are increasingly uncomfortable with the perceived necessary administration of organizational requirements, church properties, pension and insurance programs, and information handling. We are as reluctant to equate the work of the Church with "church work," as we are to see leaders solely as administrators. We want those in positions of responsibility to guide us in relating to our primary task as Christians.

We are searching for those who can rearticulate the reasons we as United Methodists have joined together in the name of Christ. This is a key role of leadership—to restate our primary purpose, to challenge each of us to be committed to that purpose, and to demonstrate the courage to be at the forefront of those moving in the required direction.

In a study of leadership, Michael Maccoby noted some important characteristics of leaders who help organizations move toward goals. He speaks of leaders in the contemporary scene, taking into account the new milieu.

What is most significant to developing leadership is three qualities . . . which correspond to the most positive attributes of the new social character: a caring, respectful and responsible attitude; flexibility about people and organizational structure; and a participative approach to management, the willingness to share power. Furthermore, they are self-aware, conscious of their weaknesses as well as strengths, concerned with self-development for themselves as well as others.[7]

The ability of The United Methodist Church to move into the future with purpose, vigor, and commitment will require leaders who have a vision of our collective future and are able to marshal our commitment and our resources. Such leadership is absolutely essential for the long-term effectiveness of our local churches and of our denomination.

The Response to Leadership

Leadership assumes followers who accept and affirm the guidance of the leader—followers who are willing to invest themselves in the vision articulated by the leader.

An organization may fail to produce quality leadership in a specific person or be unable to affirm the leadership of *any* person or group. It is extremely difficult for leaders to arise and function well in an organization where there are jealousies, prerogatives or "turf" to be protected, or that is unwilling to allow any one person to achieve prominence. Groups whose members do not have a shared sense of destiny or a fundamental trust in the purposes or activities of the organization are not likely to place much confidence or authority in leadership.

In this period of our nation's history there is a distrust of both leadership and large organizations. The tendency is to believe that neither "understands my situation." Coupled with this is the feeling that the local reality is more valid than the regional or national. As a consequence, leadership at other than the local level is considered suspect and is not given an opportunity to function creatively on behalf of all.

Leadership is an elusive phenomenon. It can be formalized by the development of authoritative positions in an organization. But leadership derives its power from free and active interchange between leader and followers. We will follow those in whom we believe and trust, those who provide us guidance and a clear statement of our tasks. We will follow them not because they occupy offices, but because they serve our needs. We all desire someone to provide conceptual and spiritual guidance, themes of action, and a description of the common purpose. Our struggle today is to find both a new statement for our collective endeavors and those who can embody it for us.

We need leaders who can rekindle our zeal to proclaim the faith and spread scriptural holiness throughout the land!

In the course of finding a new direction and marshaling our commitment, we must listen attentively for leadership. We must be sensitive to the concerns of God's work, prayerfully prepare ourselves, and be open to those who would help us move forward. New leaders may not be like those of the past. They may come from different backgrounds and perspectives. When leadership that can command our allegiance arises, we should respond *unreservedly*; neither we nor our leaders can progress if we encumber our commitment with qualifications. Quality leadership will draw us out in service and witness to the larger vision of God's purpose. Our commitment must be to join with that leadership to accomplish our common goals.

The Leadership of Precept and Example

Our leadership must not only articulate our purpose, but provide a living witness for the accomplishment of that purpose. We remember the early circuit riders not so much for what they said as for the commitment they brought to their task. It was clear that they were willing to give their very lives for the spreading of God's word, and the driving force of their example influenced others to be equally committed.

We, too, need to be willing to witness to the message of God with our words and with our lives. Such a commitment provides leadership for others to follow. Often lay people feel that the clergy are unduly concerned about the conditions or financial support systems under which they serve. Some lay people perceive that the spreading of God's Word is not the motivation of certain ministers. The precept may be correctly preached, but the living example is flawed.

Similar examples could be noted in the laity as well. It is difficult to assess the level of commitment of many Christians who are disturbed by matters peripheral to the core work of the Christian community. Reluctance to speak to another to encourage that person in spiritual growth is only one example of our tendency to separate our statement of belief from our commitment to action.

In one way or another, all of us can provide leadership to

encourage others to proclaim the faith. Those who see us actively involved will observe that we are attempting to lead by precept and example. People will not respond to us if they believe that our actions are not consistent with what we profess. In like manner, we will not follow others who do not seem to be living what they are teaching. Only as we are faithful to our beliefs can we lead. We will develop trust and confidence in our leaders only if it is clear that they are doing what they are professing.

All of us are willing to serve in Christian faith. We are willing to commit ourselves to action when we clearly understand the vision and have confidence in the challenge before us. We commit ourselves to be leaders when we are needed, and to be followers when we are needed, as we focus on God's instructions to us. Our foremost concern is that others share in God's mercy and grace. We are willing to devote ourselves to the task under appropriate leadership. Our challenge is to recognize, nurture, and encourage those who can lead us in this most fruitful mission in Christ's name.

Questions for Consideration

1. What provides our power "to spread scriptural Holiness"?
2. What is God's purpose for us as a people called United Methodists? How do we go about the task of proclaiming our faith?
3. What kind of leadership is important to us as we seek to do God's will?
4. What must be our response to the leaders in our local church and in our denomination?

CHAPTER 6

To Reform the Nation

As the early United Methodists moved across the land, their energies were devoted to the fulfillment of a single purpose: to reform the nation by spreading scriptural holiness over the land. They sought those living apart from God's grace and proclaimed the faith to them.

From the very beginning, those in connection with Wesley, Asbury, Albright, and Otterbein were seeking to reform and reshape the spiritual and moral character of the nation. Initially, the concept of reforming the nation was limited to changing the spiritual direction of the individual. Soon, however, the struggle for the individual's rights and quality of life became an integral part of the Wesleyan movement.

Our Commission for Others

United Methodism has never focused exclusively on its own needs or its own members' needs, nor has it imposed a great number of requirements for membership. Its organization was developed to provide leadership and nurture for those who joined the movement. One of its primary tasks was to strengthen the faith of those who became a part of United Methodism. This it has done well.

There was a second task: to reach others who had not received the blessings of God's grace. This involved an intense concern for the individual's spiritual health and relationship with God, together with a deep interest in the development of the individual's full potential in both this world and the next. The phrase "to reform the nation" was understood to mean spiritual reformation—not only for each person but for the total society—to address the social, economic, and political reforms needed to enable persons and society to "move on toward perfection." It is this understanding of "reforming the nation" that we will consider in this chapter.

The Gospel for the Crises of the Individual

John Wesley began his work in a troubled England. Radical changes were taking place in the social and economic fabric of his nation; industry was becoming the dominant force. Wesley saw that the Church of England was not meeting its members' spiritual needs, and he also saw that the powerful forces at work in the nation were inhibiting and destroying people's lives.

> As a social reformer, [Wesley] was against slavery, the liquor traffic, smuggling, poverty, and the trifling use of time in theater and play. He showed special concern for aiding the poor and hungry, teaching children, and visiting those in prison. Wesley stressed the impact of these and other issues on *individuals* rather than calling to task the evil *social* structures involved. Only later in England and in America did Methodist leadership inspire a social consciousness that gave content and direction to social holiness, much as Wesley had done to personal holiness.[1]

The initial emphasis in Methodism was on providing the message of the grace of God and attempting to deal with the social forces that weighed upon the individual. There are three reasons why this emphasis was dominant. First, John Wesley's impact on those "in connection" with him was enormous. He provided distinctive character for the new movement and was its principal spokesman. Methodism was personified in him. After his death, the movement began to broaden its perspective on major social issues.

Second, the early focus of the Methodist movement was on personal salvation and personal holiness. The evils of society were viewed as pitfalls that could ensnare the individual and jeopardize his or her efforts to "flee the wrath to come." Thus the early social emphasis was to prevent or at least make it less possible for the individual to sin. Through subsequent nurture in classes and congregational groups, however, some of the broader social issues began to be addressed as major problems confronting the society.

Third, in the earliest years of the Methodist, United Brethren, and Evangelical groups in this country, no organization was in a position to address and make an impact on any major social issue, although the early annual and general conferences of the clergy provided an arena for their problems in carrying out the proclamation. Soon, however, social and economic ills perceived in the nation were added to the agenda of these conferences.

A broader social conscience began to be expressed as our predecessor denominations grew and established their presence in the emerging nation. For the first one hundred years, our denomination's growth paralleled that of the nation. As a result, our United Methodist forebears found themselves in a position to serve as a conscience for the nation. No other denomination was so widely spread throughout the nation or represented as large a percentage of the population as did the United Methodist predecessors during that period. As The Protestant Episcopal Church became known as the church of the nation's leaders and of the wealthy in the "eastern establishment," so our forebears came to be known as the church of the populace. It was the church not of the factory owners, but of the family homesteads.

This wide distribution of membership meant that people in all parts of the nation were identified with and served by United Methodism. As a result, not only could United Methodists see the immediate consequences of debilitating social and economic ills, but they could sense the broad causes and impacts as well. Slavery, for example, could be seen in terms of its effects on individual slaves and owners, and also in terms of social and economic consequences for the nation. Thus, this people of God sought to reform the nation from the perspective of what was right in God's kingdom for both the individual and society.

We should keep in mind that God's expectations for the individual do not differ sharply from God's expectations for society as a whole. In the entire course of United Methodism's history, there has never been a sharp distinction made between its responsibility for individuals and its responsibility for society as a whole. For the majority of United Methodists, this has not been an either/or issue. The problem that does arise is that of keeping these two aspects in balance and creative tension. To deal solely with the individual's concerns without considering social and economic issues which affect the person's response and growth in God's grace is to deal incompletely with the reformation of the individual. On the other hand, to focus solely on social and economic issues in order to improve the lot of each person in this life, without also sharing God's revelations and instructions, is to focus on societal issues without guidance from God.

Not all United Methodists have been concerned about all social and economic issues. Major differences have existed and continue to exist within the denomination with regard to the appropriate stance or action to be taken on given issues. Nor has the denomination, in the light of history, always been correct in its judgments and viewpoints.

It has, however, been sincere in its desire to reform the nation, to eliminate those things that are wrong, and to witness to the power of God in the life of society as a whole. Our denomination has worked to change conditions and practices that affect not only its own members, but others, regardless of their religious convictions. It has struggled to right wrongs— not to enhance the position of the denomination or bring it tranquility, but because those conditions needed to be changed.

There has been disagreement within the denomination over General Conference, annual conferences, agencies, and other groups. However, we remain "in connection" to discover, through continuing conversations, what witness we must make to reform the nation.

Through our understanding of God's will, we continue to emphasize concern for the full development of the individual in relationship to God, and concern for society as a whole. Both require the continued willingness of each of us to be open to the spiritual needs and social concerns of others. If we become preoccupied with ourselves only, either as individuals or as a denomination, we cannot render our most effective service and outreach. If we continue to have strong concern for others and understand clearly what is required of us in service and action, we can remain a vital force for the redemption of individuals and the reformation of a nation.

United Methodism's Compassion for Those in Need

Response to the commission of service to others begins with attending to the immediate and personal needs of people. Just as the initial collections of Paul were gathered to help the poor, so the early Methodists' attention was focused on solving immediate problems of housing, food, and debt. Our predecessors realized that people cannot give their full attention to God while they are preoccupied with simply surviving and providing basic necessities for their families.

In the early years of our nation, society did not provide many of the services available today: education, health care, welfare. These were available only on a one-to-one basis. Churches, particularly the United Methodists of the time, urged their members to be concerned and involved in providing such help.

Racism

While the needs of individuals were being met through personal service, it was becoming increasingly apparent that some major social problems of the nation needed to be a)dressed. The first of these issues to occupy the denomination was slavery. Especially in the northern states, slavery was considered immoral. The issue was hotly debated both in the nation and in the church. Both sides developed support within the denomination, and the controversy divided Methodism in 1844.

Through its official positions and actions, United Methodism has sought to reform both itself and the nation. Congregations and individual members are urged to move toward that perfection in love which acknowledges that all persons are of equal worth and dignity. The issue of slavery was decided in the political arena through war. In the last few decades, the issue has become segregation and racism. To this day, racism has not been completely eradicated within the nation or within the denomination.

Society is moving toward yet another phase in its under-standing of racism. In the first phase—slavery—blacks were considered inferior, created to do menial work. This phase lasted until the conclusion of the Civil War in 1865.

In the second phase—the segregated society—whites believed blacks to be at a different (lower) stage of development. As a result, the mixing of the races was considered bad for both and contrary to the law of God. This phase lasted until about 1940.

The third phase—the inclusive society—has as its dominant theme the conviction that blacks and whites are equal; that any differences are the result of white racism and could be overcome by remedial programs such as affirmative action in jobs and protection through legislation. This phase is still in effect.

But we are now beginning to enter a fourth phase—the pluralistic society. In this phase the conviction is held that there are distinct cultural and ethnic groups in the society, which have the right and even the duty to preserve their own identities. Therefore, we have the call to prepare materials that reflect more than one cultural heritage, and in more than one language. What effect this will have on national unity is still to be determined; our future direction is unclear.[2]

It is important for those of us in the church to understand how these forces will affect both the nation and our denomination. Our task is to provide a theological framework for understanding and undergirding society and to provide direction in light of our understanding of God's injunctions. As a denomination, we are presently dealing with racism in concepts that relate to the third phase and are not able to provide the needed leadership.

The denomination must continue to struggle with this issue and continue to move toward the Christian position. Its goal must be to reform itself and the nation so that all persons may share equally and be received fully and unreservedly into all our associations with one another.

Education

Education has been another primary emphasis of United Methodists. Our concern began with Wesley's desire that the clergy and leadership of the church be well informed concerning the Christian faith. Strong emphasis was placed also on the availability of Christian materials to undergird the proclamation of the Word and the nurture of the individual. It is not surprising, therefore, that the first agency established was a publishing concern.

When it became apparent that the individual's full potential and growth in Christian faith could be enhanced through education, attention was given to the establishment of schools. At first these were academies, or high school-level institutions. Then colleges and theological schools for the training of clergy were founded. The primary goal was to provide training and education for as many as possible, not only those who could afford to attend. Persons with ability were encouraged and assisted in attending United Methodist colleges. These educational institutions were a major factor in developing the intellectual and moral leadership of the nation during the denomination's first one-hundred-fifty years in this country. In a very significant way, this emphasis on education did bring about a major transformation, or reformation, in the life of the nation. United Methodists provided education for many who otherwise would not have had such opportunities.

In addition, the denomination sought to serve specific educational needs which other parts of society could not or would not serve. Elementary schools were provided in some communities where neither the white nor the black schools would accept children of racially mixed marriages. Advanced education was made available to and affordable by many blacks when many schools could not or would not accept them. A medical college was established for blacks at a time when they were excluded from all other medical schools in this country. Schools were begun for Hispanic and Indian students.

Throughout its history The United Methodist Church has had a strong commitment to education. This is an example of the denomination's response to a need—a response which led the nation in the development of its educational programs; a response which provided training and moral perspective for many men and women who moved into positions of leadership in education, health, government, law, and religion. We will never be able to fully document the enormous influence United

Methodism has had on American society through its emphasis on education. There is no question that the denomination has thereby helped shape and reform the nation.

Alcohol, Tobacco, and Drug Use

Other examples abound. For example, United Methodists have led in the establishment of all kinds of health care institutions and have been in the forefront of the creation of the major health care delivery systems in place today. Through the years, we also have provided key leadership for reform on such major social issues as alcohol, tobacco, and drug abuse. Perhaps the most dramatic impact was evidenced by the Methodist role in the temperance movement which led to the passage of the Prohibition Amendment to the United States Constitution. Although the amendment was repealed, United Methodists retain a strong official position concerning the use of alcohol. We remain one of the leaders in dispensing information about the harmful effects of alcohol, tobacco products, and drugs.

Economics

With the full industrial development of the United States, our predecessor denominations devoted considerable attention and energy to economic issues. The social gospel movement, which developed in the late nineteenth and early twentieth centuries, initially dealt with economic issues. This had a major influence on United Methodism. Early and progressive stands were taken on labor laws, labor unions, equitable wages, and other matters. Often embroiled in controversy over issues taken for granted today, United Methodism struggled to insure the rights and needs of the individual, in a nation dominated by major industrial and money interests.

The first Social Creed passed by the Methodist Episcopal Church in 1916 reflects its positions on economic issues. It states, in part:

The Methodist Episcopal Church stands—
For equal rights and complete justice for all men in all stations of life.

For the principle of conciliation and arbitration in industrial dissensions.

For the protection of the worker from dangerous machinery, occupational diseases, injuries, and mortality.

For the abolition of child labor.

For the regulation of the conditions of labor for women as shall safeguard the physical and moral health of the community. . . .

For the highest wage that each industry can afford, and for the most equitable division of the products of industry that can ultimately be devised.

Social Creed

The Methodist Episcopal Church, South, and the Evangelical United Brethren Church, as well as many other Protestant groups, adopted social creeds. Through the years, our denomination has continued to express its concern for a broad range of issues. Each annual conference expresses its opinion on issues, and the General Conference establishes the official position of The United Methodist Church by passing resolutions and then commending them to the denomination for study and action. A part of *The Book of Discipline* includes a major section entitled "Social Principles." This statement sets forth the position of the denomination on (1) the natural world, (2) the nurturing community, (3) the social community, (4) the economic community, (5) the political community, and (6) the world community.

Following the custom established in 1916, General Conference also develops a Social Creed, a major affirmation of our position on social and economic issues. It is approved by General Conference with the recommendation that it be emphasized regularly in every local church. It is worthy of study. The Social Creed adopted in 1980 is reproduced here in full to emphasize the full range of concerns addressed by The United Methodist Church.

We believe in God, Creator of the world; and in Jesus Christ the Redeemer of creation. We believe in the Holy Spirit, through whom we acknowledge God's gifts, and we repent of our sin in misusing these gifts to idolatrous ends.

We affirm the natural world as God's handiwork and dedicate ourselves to its preservation, enhancement, and faithful use by humankind.

We joyfully receive, for ourselves and others, the blessings of community, sexuality, marriage, and the family.

We commit ourselves to the rights of men, women, children, youth, young adults, the aging, and those with handicapping conditions; to improvement of the quality of life; and to the rights and dignity of racial, ethnic, and religious minorities.

We believe in the right and duty of persons to work for the good of themselves and others, and in the protection of their welfare in so doing; in the rights to property as a trust from God, collective bargaining, and responsible consumption; and in the elimination of economic and social distress.

We dedicate ourselves to peace throughout the world and to the rule of justice and law among nations.

We believe in the present and final triumph of God's Word in human affairs, and gladly accept our commission to manifest the life of the gospel in the world. Amen.[3]

There is no question that United Methodism has and does express itself on social and economic issues that affect its members and all other persons. This is a part of its task. We continue to deal with injustice and inhumanity that weigh against human growth and development. In so doing we seek to make known God's will and provide a social and economic setting in which each person can grow in relationship to God. We attempt to eliminate those factors that separate us from God and from one another. In order to reshape and reform the nation in accordance with God's commandments, to be vital as Christians and United Methodists, we must pledge ourselves to continuing encounters with social and economic issues.

Crises in Our Third Century

The period we are now entering in our national and world history reflects a radical change in industrial and social life much like the change that occurred in Wesley's lifetime. In John Wesley's time, the predominantly agricultural society and economy (the first wave) gave way to an industrial society and economy (the second wave). The new period we are entering is described in various ways—as a postindustrial age, an electronic age, the time of the computer or microcircuit, or as the "third wave." The lack of a single descriptive term is another indication that this new period is just beginning.

Major changes are taking place in the economic structure. The major heavy industries in this nation—steel, automobiles, machine tools, and heavy goods manufacturing—are no longer prospering. Employment is shifting away from the making of products to the processing of information, much of it electronically, and to the providing of services. As a consequence, employment is shifting from traditional "blue collar" jobs to service or skilled technical positions.

The influence of these changes on economic and social patterns is profound. All about us we see change and transition in small adjustments and in major sweeps. We see the impact of these changes on individuals as they adjust to new work environments and skill requirements, relocate following plant closings, deal with inflation, and try to acquire the information and flexibility demanded by the complexities of daily living. On the national and world scenes, there is poverty, lack of educational and other opportunities, racism, drug and alcohol abuse, and new and violent forms of war. With the development of television, we not only read about these issues, but we literally see people who are starving to death, intense injury caused by natural disasters, consequences of disease and poverty, and the inhumanity of terrorism and war. So frequently do we see these events that we become immune to their personal and social impact.

The United Methodist Church is still at work at many places to reform the nation and the world with its service in God's name. On the local level, congregations work to alleviate suffering in countless communities across the nation; they seek to support those trying to change regulations, customs, and laws to create a more humane world. In the aggregate, these small acts of Christian love have enormous power.

On the denominational level The United Methodist Church is addressing similar social concerns. It provides relief in places of immediate tragedy through the alleviation of physical suffering, disease, and hunger. It also addresses the basic underlying issues of hunger, poverty, ill health, and lack of education. The denomination speaks the Christian witness by making its position known in the legislatures of this nation. While it does not always accomplish all it pursues, the church continues to work at the task.

Many of the issues are the same as those present at the beginning of our history. Some have taken new forms or require new responses and new solutions because of technological changes. Some issues are new because the world has changed and new knowledge is available to us.

But like the early United Methodists, we still speak of the need to eliminate poverty. We speak of the inequitable distribution of wealth and the exploitation of people. We are still confronted by the evils of war. We speak of the need for peace with justice. We now view war not only in terms of actual conflict, but also in terms of increasing militarism, the build-up and distribution of armaments, the potential for nuclear devastation, and the development of space as a new frontier for military conquest and control.

It is a new time for our nation and our world. It is a new century of work for our denomination. There is no question that the church must continue to inform and reform itelf as it seeks to do the same for the nation. Social, economic, and political forces at work in the world are creating a whole new set of issues for the society of the third wave, which are necessarily becoming a part of the United Methodist agenda, whether we like it or not.

The key question is whether we as United Methodists will be able to respond adequately to these issues. The charge to be of service to others in the name of Christ remains, although the context for this service has changed and will continue to change. We must be willing to make the necessary adjustments so that United Methodism can remain relevant and effective in light of our changing environment. To fail to continue to reform the nation according to God's principles is to diminish the witness possible for United Methodism in its next century; it is to turn away from one of the guiding purposes of our founders. Our work for the reformation of the society remains one of the most important ways in which we can serve.

Our Response of Service to the Nation and to the World

As United Methodists, we have been known as a people concerned about others. We have, from the beginning, proclaimed Christ as Savior to all who would respond. The requirements to be "in connection," have always been secondary to the requirements of a full and complete response to God.

So, too, have we been known as a people willing to serve others in any way possible. We have joined with other denominations to bring about change. We have sought new solutions to pressing problems. Help for the suffering and encouragement of the individual have taken priority over the prerogatives of the denomination, for we have been a people willing to serve. As we reflect on our history, we must consider how well we are prepared to serve and witness in our third century.

The Lessons of History and the Tensions of Today

As committed Christians we are in the center of a dynamic world. As United Methodists we believe that the commitment which one makes as a Christian requires a deep and complete personal response to God. As part of that response, we redirect our own personal life and seek to perfect our relationship with God. We complete our response when we are of service to others. This outreach requires that we present to others the message of God's salvation and grace. We are to be of service, help where we can, and change those things which demean, demoralize, and diminish other persons.

When we enter into outreach and service, we are entering arenas where there are tensions and struggles. We encounter those who prefer that no changes be made, perhaps because they benefit from conditions as they are, perhaps because they are not aware of the good that may come from change, or perhaps because they simply resist giving up their present patterns of activity and thought.

Even so, there are times when we as individuals, as local congregations, as annual conferences, and as a total denomination must become engaged in a struggle over an issue or on behalf of a fundamental human right. As we review the lessons of our church history, we note that we sometimes have made inadequate or inappropriate responses. In retrospect, we see that we made decisions that were ill informed or premature. As costly as those decisions may have been, and while we regret our errors, we must affirm that those involved were earnest in their desire to serve.

We can note other issues on which United Methodism chose not to speak, and we can only speculate as to the reasons in each instance. In some cases the denomination has refrained from speaking until an issue was largely decided in the broad arena of public opinion. Again, in retrospect, we can note instances where our denomination has failed. History teaches us that some positions taken have been costly. The Methodist Episcopal Church was divided by the issue of slavery and not reunited for nearly one hundred years. Controversies over the rights of bishops and lay representation in the conferences led to another separation in 1830. Within the denomination today, there are differing viewpoints on a number of social and economic issues. We lack complete consensus on ways to accomplish many tasks and on the positions to be taken on many important social issues. Yet United Methodists remain "in connection," seeking to speak a common word to our society.

Tension develops among United Methodists, in part, because we are a large church, representing all segments of the nation. Theological stances of individuals and congregations vary. We differ on method as well as content in relation to an issue. Some United Methodists, intensely interested and involved in a specific issue, cannot understand why others do not share their viewpoint or the strength of their conviction. Some United Methodists support formal, institutional responses, while others prefer less structured solutions. Thus there are tensions—some creative, some destructive.

Yet we remain "in connection." We struggle with the issues because this is part of our commitment. We strive for a common mind, and when we can reach agreement, we rejoice and seek to live out our decisions in effective service. When we cannot reach agreement, we try to understand one another and move in whatever direction and with whatever resolve we can collectively authorize. We stay in conversation because the strengths that hold us together remain stronger than the tensions that would pull us apart. We are joined under the banner of United Methodism because of our conviction that together, we can best serve and proclaim.

The lessons of history affirm that love and understanding ultimately are victorious. This is true whether we are attempting to change a major force in our society or whether we are seeking a consensus within the denomination. We hold our discussions in an atmosphere of love and mutual respect, while witnessing to what we understand to be best for all in the sight of God. We generally abide by the decisions of the majority in our churches and our conferences. Where there is disappointment, we seek to moderate and temper opinions.

One word of caution is in order for United Methodists, as well as for every other group. Throughout history there have been individuals and groups who, in attempting to win acceptance of their point of view, have lost sight of the larger vision of God's will and purpose for individuals, the denomination, and the society. The needs and rights of individuals have sometimes been subordinated in the heat of discussion, and winning has become more important than the issue involved or the persons affected. Victory has been hollow, or even lost because of the damage done to other groups or persons.

Intense as a conviction may be, or as desirable as the end result may be, techniques and actions that override the purpose for which we come together in the name of Christ should not be utilized. We dare not demean others, even those on whose behalf we are struggling. Within the Christian community we struggle to witness to God's love and concern. We cannot do this if, in times of intense debate, we choose approaches that are contrary to our fundamental witness to God's grace and love. The strength of our faith must be clearly present as we present our position, and as we witness to that position through love and service.

Institutions That Enable and Those That Encumber

We live in a large and complex society. The complexity is increasing as we become part of a highly integrated, interdependent world economy and social structure. When we consider only our own national government, we can become lost in the intricacy of bureaus, departments, divisions, commissions, and laws and regulations. As we search for understanding, we see additional layers of bureaucracy at state and local levels. Are there parts of this enormous structure that are no longer needed? Parts that are redundant? Do all the bureaucratic components effectively carry out their assigned responsibilities on behalf of the whole citizenry?

The same questions come to mind in considering our denomination. It is large and complex, with organizations, programs, and interests at the national, regional, conference, district, and local levels. We can become lost amid all the agencies, divisions, commissions, committees, and legislation and regulations. Each component was established to deal with a significant issue or concern that confronted the church as it sought to proclaim and serve. The publishing enterprise, for example, grew out of the need for an educated laity and clergy. Educational and health care institutions were established to fill a need not being met by society. The denomination's missionary agency was begun as a way to facilitate the recruiting, sending, and supporting of missionaries. Through the years we have developed a large and complex organization to carry forward God's work.

How can we keep the message of Christ vital? What are the criteria by which we make decisions concerning future institutional needs? How do we determine and assess factors vital and central to our task? How do we discover which factors are peripheral today? Earl D. C. Brewer describes the need to address the bureaucracy issue: "The mere maintenance of the bureaucracy of United Methodism, from local to general levels, has become an absorbing mission of the body, capable of drowning enthusiasm for Christian mission. . . . Can the denomination move beyond routine maintenance of bureaucratic organization toward the spiritual, missional dynamic of a biblical faith working through appropriate structures? The issue is critical for the future."[4]

This is a crucial issue for two reasons. First, we must ask whether all we are doing today can stand scrutiny as actions that extend the Christian message of salvation and nurture those who respond. Are our activities and institutions accomplishing our task as Christians and as United Methodists? Are we devoting our energies to reforming the nation?

Second, the bureaucracy issue is crucial because our response will determine the way we relate to the individual and to the world in the future. If we now have an institution through which we can make Christ known to countless persons and serve human need, we will develop renewed vigor for the future. If, however, we uncritically support institutions and programs that devote much of their energies to their own maintenance and survival, then the church will not achieve major growth and outreach.

While these statements have been put in terms of the total denomination, the issue is just as critical for local churches, annual conferences, and the many institutions and programs of the church. Is what we are doing enabling, or is it encumbering the accomplishment of our basic task? That is the question we must answer responsibly. Earl Brewer sums it up for us.

The United Methodist Church, as well as other denominations, has too frequently succumbed to structural rigidity and fundamentalism, rather than witnessing in freedom to God's Spirit in the world. . . . Does Methodism's structural fundamentalism indicate that we consider adherence to the letter of the law more significant than following the witness of the Spirit, especially if it leads to raising questions about church structures? This spiritual malaise is seen also in the lack of daring and fervor to explore new avenues to God's altar and new visions of mission. There is, rather, a tendency to be satisfied with the defense and maintenance of existing structures and programs.[5]

This is a pressing issue. How will we respond to the enormous changes that are occurring in the social and economic structures around us? It becomes increasingly clear that all levels of the denomination must adapt in order to remain relevant and of service. *If we do not find new methods, if we do not restate old truths for the emerging age, we will be left behind as a monument to the past.*

But mere survival is not our goal. If we still believe that we must reform the nation, attune it to the needs of all people, and form appropriate responses to major social issues, then we must, with candor and courage, test our own institution for its ability to serve and remain relevant. We must affirm and strengthen those activities, programs, institutions, and organizations that enable us to proclaim the faith in the present age and in the future. Those activities that are encumbering our performance of essential tasks must be changed and invigorated for new work, or they must be discontinued, with grateful appreciation for past service.

It is not easy to review one's own work. It is a little like cleaning out a closet. We find things we remember with great affection, but which serve no useful purpose and now occupy space valued at a premium. Yet we are reluctant to discard them to make way for more useful items. But neither local churches nor annual conferences, nor the denomination can afford to keep accumulating things not central to our vital message. It will not be easy to reach a consensus about what is needed and what is not, but if we keep before us the ultimate standard by which we gauge our purpose and activity, quick and ready agreement may be ours. Our success in spreading scriptural holiness and reforming the nation will depend on how well we perform the difficult task of self-examination and revitalization.

To Serve with Vigor—Our Commitment to Action

Reforming the nation involves the spiritual conversion of individuals. It also involves changing those factors in society that demean, dehumanize, or limit realization of the full potential of persons.

To fulfill our responsibility, we must witness actively. We must strive to improve the social situation in which each person lives. We must seek to overcome both the immediate effects and the underlying causes of major social ills. Our active involvement is one way we proclaim our faith. This takes us through four steps.

1. We must become aware of the forces operating in society. When we understand the economic, political, and social

dynamics at work, we can more clearly perceive their effects. We can detect which factors allow people to move toward perfecting relationships with God and with others, and which inhibit or destroy this possibility. We can isolate the issues that require our active witness and energies. We can proclaim our Christian faith as individuals and in groups by seeking to redress the wrongs and inequities of society.

2. With the issues defined, we can work for a consensus of opinion that will bring about a commitment to act. We must begin with our own commitment to address an issue or an injustice. We can then enlist the help of others, both within and outside the denomination, to develop a broader awareness of the issue and the desired solution. When we reach a consensus, we can move with purpose and resolve, committed to action.

3. The commitment to action motivates us to bring about the needed change. The type of action needed will depend on the issue. But agreement about the nature of the injustice or social problem and the type of action needed is not enough. We must carry out the action to correct the wrong. If we are to enhance the lives of individuals, improve society, and reform the nation, we must be committed to bring about needed changes.

4. We act to fulfill our purpose as Christians. We are motivated by our desire to provide the best possible environment in which individuals can respond to and receive the proclamation of the faith and the assurance of God's blessing. If we are not working toward this ultimate purpose, we as Christians will not be distinguished from all others working for social reform, however effective and well meaning they may be.

We are United Methodists, working to reform the nation because we believe that God has made possible the redemption of each person and of society. We confront issues not because they are wrong in the eyes of society, but because they are wrong in the sight of God. We struggle to reform the nation in order to affirm the individual and to bring to fruition the kingdom of God!

Our effort is not simply to make technical or organizational adjustments. We must focus society and all its parts on the purposes of God and the enhancement of all people. This is indeed a radical reformation, for it calls into question many of the things we now do and support—as individuals, as a church, and as a nation. All that we do is to be seen from a new perspective, for now we are to assess our activities and those of society by the criteria of God's purposes and will.

This requires our full commitment to serve in God's name with resolve and vigor. We proclaim the faith to bring the knowledge of God's saving grace to more persons. We nurture and build up the Church in order to develop the full potential of each individual and to spread scriptural holiness throughout the land. We witness and serve in order to provide the social environment in which all persons can fully realize their worth as individuals. When we have accomplished these things, we truly will have reformed the nation!

Questions for Consideration

1. Why has United Methodism, from its beginnings, placed an emphasis on social concerns and on reforming the nation?
2. How will we, as United Methodists, be able to develop adequate responses, in God's name, to the social issues of today and tomorrow?
3. How can we keep the message of Christ vital in our complex society in the future?
4. What must we, as United Methodists, do to witness and serve in the reformation of the nation?

CHAPTER 7

Into Our Third Century

All of us have significant points at which we pause to reflect upon our life and project plans for our future. When we are young, we reflect on the family that nurtured us, but we are eager to move on and do not have much perspective or depth in our contemplation of our past. As we grow older, the observances of decade milestones serve as occasions for reflection. When we turn forty, we view our life as in mid-course. At that point we have had enough experience to reflect deeply about the past and to foresee the future into which we are about to move.

So it is now with United Methodism. In 1984 we will observe the bicentennial of our denomination's formal organizational beginning in this country. The United Methodist Church now has had a significant span of life experience upon which to reflect. We, also, must foresee what we will be called to do in God's name as we enter our third century.

For Two Centuries, Proclaiming Grace and Freedom

From the time of the Christmas Conference of 1784, we United Methodists have been proclaiming God's grace. John Wesley stressed that we receive this gift of love through Christ by our acceptance in faith. We have the assurance that God acted in love to restore us. We have the further assurance that we can respond to that love and "move on to perfection" in our relationship with God. Because of these two assurances, we understand that our task is to bring others into this same restored and perfectable relationship with God in love. By stressing these emphases we became known as the people of the assurance. Because of our assurance, we United Methodists have known that our task—indeed, our obligation—is to share the faith with as many persons as possible. We must proclaim the faith, nurture those who come into this new relationship with God, and serve those who are in need. Through proclamation and service, United Methodists have sought to meet the needs both of individuals and of society.

We have chosen to be "in connection" with one another to accomplish these tasks. As individuals we have joined with groups and congregations under the United Methodist banner to share and develop our Christian faith and witness. We have joined together further in annual conferences and as a total denomination to find the concerted purpose and direction that will best enable us to serve in proclaiming our faith.

Our denomination was born in a time of significant social turmoil and stress. John Wesley helped to recast the religious experience for many persons, in an England that was undergoing major economic and social changes. United Methodism began on this continent while a new nation was emerging, economic patterns were unsettled, and great numbers of people were migrating to this new land. Francis Asbury, Philip Otterbein, Jacob Albright, and those in association with them sought to help individuals find a faith relationship with God amid all the changes taking place. They brought assurance in a time of transition and stress. Proclaiming the assurance of God was of great significance during that period.

Throughout much of our history we have helped individuals and society respond to rapidly changing and stressful conditions. United Methodism's ability to focus on people's needs enabled it to respond to and move with the growing population. A high level of creativity can be seen in the methods used to relate God's assurance in the changing scene. *United Methodism did not need to defend old forms or practices.* Instead, it looked for and found the most viable ways to proclaim its faith and to be of service.

In recent decades, different changes and stresses have confronted the nation. United Methodism has not been able to deal constructively with all these new factors, for the denomination has been increasingly preoccupied with maintaining established institutions, programs, methods, and organizations. The creativity and flexibility needed to respond to the factors that impact individuals and society today are not readily apparent. Conservation has supplanted creativity. Caution has replaced commitment. Preoccupation with the present has outweighed proclamation for the future.

Let me cite one example. The decline in the number of members in the denomination has been widely discussed in recent years. Indeed, a net gain in membership has not been registered for any single year since the merger in 1968 formed The United Methodist Church. We hear such statements as, "The leadership must address the problem of membership decline."

Unfortunately, we have already addressed the issue of membership *decline*. We have focused on (1) clearing membership rolls (partly because of inactive and unaccounted for members and partly because of a desire to reduce the amount of money apportioned to the local church), (2) handling procedures for those who transfer, and (3) removing names of those who have died, withdrawn, or otherwise been lost to our ministry.

Now we need to focus our attention on the issue of membership *increase!* We must move from institutional concerns of membership (especially in terms of how many persons are needed to support the budget) to personal faith concerns, not only of active members, but of inactive members and nonmembers as well. Our emphasis must turn from our own internal concerns as a large complex organization, whether as a congregation or as a denomination, to the personal concerns of those who need to hear the proclamation of God's action through Christ!

To preserve and consolidate is not our call. It is not enough. The history of our denomination demonstrates that when it has lost itself in proclamation and service, it has found a creativity and power that led to its own growth. When there was a clarity of purpose to reach out to others, there was a vitality and commitment that enabled it to respond effectively to spiritual hungers and physical needs.

In recent years, many people have begun to focus on problems and tension within the denomination. Various groups, with good motives, have emphasized one viewpoint to the detriment or possible exclusion of others. We have looked at the problems, blemishes, differences, and faults within the organization, rather than outward, at our purposes and goals.

Different perspectives within the denomination can be productive for the total purpose of the denomination, if developed with constraint and love. Dialogue between those who would give primacy to evangelism and those who would emphasize social action can enhance creativity and produce new insights. In like manner, tensions between our diversities and our singularity of purpose can create energy and motivation for action.

But if we do not see these tensions in the light of our being bound together as a people of God, we run the risk of tearing ourselves asunder. In the absence of the larger perspective of our Christian faith and our unique Wesleyan heritage, a small rift may grow to a dangerous point. We must understand anew that we are "in connection" with one another. We did not join together as United Methodists in order to serve the particularized needs of one group, or to establish one perspective to the exclusion or detriment of others. We joined "in connection" with one another to proclaim the faith and to be of service in the multitude of ways available to us as a large denomination.

Tensions arise from lack of a clear, mutually agreed upon goal for the present and future. There are those who focus on only a part of the denomination's ministry. At worst, they do so to diminish or destroy other segments; at best, to gain ascendency in viewpoint and position for their particular concern. Without a clearly perceived goal for the total denomination, affirmed in love, our focus is easily led astray to the limited works of segmented groups within the church. Our focus must be on the ministry of proclamation and service, rather than on the denomination's internal stresses and tensions. We must search for solutions in light of God's broader objective of redemption, rather than from our own limited perspectives.

The power of early United Methodism came from its

understanding and love of its witness for Christ. United Methodists were absolutely convinced of the power of their message of assurance. They were confident and optimistic about God's work. From this came the group's motivation "to share itself with the world." *Could it be that much of our present hesitancy, or difficulty in sharing ourselves with the world, arises from our lack of confidence that we ourselves fully experience the assurance of God's witness and power in our lives, as persons, as congregations, and as a denomination?*

The search for unity and purpose is not a goal in and of itself. It is important only as a way for The United Methodist Church to develop the resolve to discuss, to agree upon, and to live out a creative future. We seek a course of action to which the denomination will be committed. We seek a new direction for United Methodism, similar to that which it undertook when it moved "to reform the continent and to spread scriptural Holiness over these Lands."

The People of the Assurance for the Future

The United Methodist Church stands poised at the beginning of its third century. A bicentennial celebration alone will not create a significant watershed of experience for the denomination. But such a celebration does present an occasion to reflect on who we were, who we are, and who we wish to be as a people of God. The observance of the bicentennial presents an opportunity to examine our life "in connection" with one another.

Many persons within United Methodism today are looking for marching orders for the future. Some see the denomination as aged and inflexible. Others are trying to find focal points around which to marshall their energies. All are looking for evidence that we are indeed a "people of the assurance" for the future.

In a real sense, the question being asked today is this: Can a two-hundred-year-old denomination achieve a renewed sense of purpose and sufficient vitality and commitment to enable it to witness to God's assurance in today's world? The answer being heard from many sources is that, indeed, United

Methodism can do this. But first it must affirm that sense of assurance which leads to a spiritual revival and a commitment to reach out to others.

Individual United Methodists, congregations, and the denomination as a whole must again be able to proclaim the assurance that God acts for the redemption of all people. We are once again experiencing enormous change and stress in our society. We can only speculate about the full nature of the changes, and the scale now is not just national, but worldwide. In the midst of conflicting and often contradictory technologies, social patterns, and economic trends, stands the individual who is attempting to discover his or her appropriate role in our complex world.

That is why words of assurance are so important. We know that in times of personal stress we seek solace and guidance from our Christian faith. We return to the Church to hear again the testimony of God's action on our behalf. We seek out the community of believers for support and strength. Together as a community of faith, we act to meet the immediate needs of persons and to serve the society in which we live. Our Christian faith enables us to deal with life's crises and to understand its ultimate values.

Our challenge today is to continue as the people of the assurance, to affirm individuals in God's grace, and to reform and change where needed. *If we do not proclaim, sustain, and serve with great assurance, then we fail.*

God's assurances and promises are still before us. From the beginning of creation to the promises of continuing new possibilities, God has been and is confronting us with great opportunities. The great potential for the future is seen in the vision and promise of the book of Revelation.

Then I saw a new heaven and a new earth; for the first heaven and the first earth had passed away, and the sea was no more. And I saw the holy city, new Jerusalem, coming down out of heaven from God . . . and I heard a loud voice from the throne saying, "Behold, the dwelling of God is with men. He will dwell with them, and they shall be his people, and God himself will be with them" (Rev. 21:1-4 RSV).

How will we respond to this vision? How will we meet people's needs? New forms of ministry will not grow out of structures and organizational forms, but from our commitment to our tasks as Christians. Creative ministry will result from our efforts to share the assurance of God with those who live in our world.

United Methodists first must receive God's grace, and then they must proclaim the message of God, receiving all who respond. We are to make known the power of God's salvation made available through Christ. Wesley and our early forebears in this nation understood this well. They were able to establish a strong faith commitment from which to provide outreach and service to others. This commitment in the congregation became the essential point for proclamation, nurture, and service. They were careful also to strive to maintain these Christian communities as strong, viable, and purposeful.

How can we continue as the people of the assurance in our third century? What must we personally affirm? What must our local churches and denomination do if we are to proclaim the faith and serve in God's name?

Let me suggest some primary characteristics our church must have if we are to continue as the people of assurance, if we are to be a vital force in proclaiming God's message in our third century. The methods and techniques required may be familiar, or they may be radically different from methods used today.

1. First, as United Methodists, we must be fully convinced of the reality of God's gracious activity in our lives. Each person's commitment to Christ should be sincere and profound. We dare not affirm our Christian principles lightly, or play at the business of being religious. The years ahead will require of each of us a deep personal commitment, well informed through our study of Scriptures and our prayer life. Such a personal commitment to Christ will bring forth a disciplined life of witness and service. We make a serious mistake if we do not clearly appreciate this need for a profound personal affirmation. We cannot embody or proclaim the assurance of God convincingly to others unless we fully commit ourselves to Christ. As a faith community, we must help one another

develop, as fully as possible, those disciplines that deepen our faith and enrich our witness.

It cannot be overemphasized that *the power of The United Methodist Church issues from the faith commitment of its members.* Programs, structures, and organizations may channel and focus that power, but they cannot create it. The starting point for all we do will be the reality and strength of our individual conviction of God's gracious activity in our lives.

2. We must become well informed about our Christian faith and our United Methodist heritage. Thus we will come to understand the vitality of Christian experience through the years and appreciate the unique contribution United Methodism has made. Knowledge of our background will provide us with a firm basis for understanding our heritage and the basis of our unity in purpose and action. This knowledge gives us our sense of identity and is essential.

3. The strength and vitality of the local congregation must be assured. It is in this community of believers that we join for worship, nurture, and service. Here we testify to one another concerning our faith commitment; here we encourage and nurture one another; and here we come to understand what our collective ministry in the name of United Methodism should be. Here we develop the strengths and commitments to be "in connection" for witness and service, in our communities and throughout the world.

As the Wesleyan societies did in the past, so the local congregation should provide a home base for spiritual growth, development, and outreach in the future. As it becomes a strong gathered community, the local congregation will find that its response to God's love and mercy lies in loving, caring, witnessing, and serving. As is true with individuals, so it is with congregations—the assurance of God cannot be convincingly proclaimed or embodied if we are not dedicated to Christ. The local congregation must be strong to make our collective witness strong. This must be accomplished, even if we must postpone other activities.

4. We must develop a clear consensus as to who we are as a people of God and what we are called to do in the future. It is absolutely essential that we have a statement of purpose and

direction. If we clearly understand our message, we can provide convincing witness to others. Our testimony and resolve will be sure only if our understanding of our task is sure. The United Methodist Church will speak with cogency, eloquence, power, and assurance, if its vision of the future is clear. What a testimony we could make!

5. All lay people must be urged and enabled to develop their full potential for witness and service. As in the early days of United Methodism, outreach and nurture cannot wait until ministers are available. Lay people must assume responsibility for an expanded range of tasks. Witnessing to one's faith and being in service should be an integral part of the Christian experience. We must marshal the extraordinary power of our laity to share their Christian experience with others. The local congregation should provide the setting for lay training and support.

6. Ordained ministers must be enabled to direct their attention to the major functions of Word, Sacrament, and Order. For these specific tasks, they have been set aside, or ordained, by the denomination. The clergy's attention should be on fulfilling these tasks and on enabling lay people to accomplish lay tasks. The clergy can provide leadership in establishing the spiritual tone and character of the local church and in guiding its witness and service.

7. We must be open to the development and guidance of strong, committed leadership. Whenever we can, we ourselves must be willing to assume the role of leader. We must utilize our talents and skills to enhance the life of the Church. However modest or great the task, if our abilities can be used effectively to proclaim or to serve in God's name, then we must respond.

We must be open, also, to the leadership of others. There is no question that our congregations, conferences, and entire denomination stand in need of vital, visionary leadership. Those who are committed to Christ and called to roles of leadership should receive our support. They are the persons who will present the vision, lead the way, and marshal our energies. Our response must be one of acceptance and encouragement. We must be willing to sense the call for responsible action and receive the gift of leadership as a part of God's response to our need.

8. Service to others must be a distinctive outgrowth of our Christian commitment. Service and action are an extension of our response to God in Christ. The conditions and nature of our service in the future may change, but our commitment to serve those in need must remain strong.

9. We must carefully examine our lives "in connection" as United Methodists, to insure that the programs, activities, customs, organizations, and institutions we have developed will continue to provide the most fruitful and effective witness to God's grace and saving power. We dare not allow our attention to be diverted by attempting to shore up and sustain activities and institutions of diminishing worth and increasing irrelevance. We must assess all our actions candidly to determine whether they help or hinder us in accomplishing our primary purpose. We must focus upon our central task—proclaiming the faith in Jesus Christ. All that we do must be assessed in light of that criterion.

10. Above all else, as United Methodists, we must proclaim our faith! We must feel an impelling conviction to go and share, to make known the assurances of God. We cannot delegate this responsibility to others.

For two hundred years, United Methodism has been a significant force in spreading Christianity throughout the world. While the need clearly has not diminished, the environment in which the message is to be conveyed has changed. Old opportunities have vanished and new ones have arisen.

Those who founded United Methodism saw the task, understood their responsibilities, and responded by committing themselves unreservedly. They proclaimed their belief in God's assurance as seen through Christ. They built up the Church and strengthened the fellowship of believers. They witnessed and served both society and individuals.

The same challenge is before us today. A nation and a world stand in need of our witness and service in the name of Christ. We must develop a community of faith in which all persons are restored in love and mutual caring. We are called to serve others at their point of need. How will we respond in the years ahead?

Our foremost call is to declare again the assurance that God is a loving, seeking, redeeming God, who reaches out to us continually. We affirm that God's mercy is available to us and to all others through Christ. We believe that we can be perfected in love. The power of United Methodism flourished as it sought to carry this message to each individual and to society as a whole.

The beginning of our third century poses serious concerns and issues for the individual and for society. For United Methodists, it can be a time of conserving and holding on to that which we already have. Or it can be a time of challenge, opportunity, risk, and creative response to new situations and needs. Our choice is clear. Either we choose how we will respond, or the passage of time will determine our fate for us.

For the future, we must continue to be the people of the assurance. In response to God's gracious activity in our lives, we must witness and serve in Christ's name. This is our task. How well we accomplish it in our third centruy will determine the future of The United Methodist Church, for all that we do must issue from our determination and commitment to proclaim the faith.

Questions for Consideration

1. What must we do to experience fully the assurance of God's grace and love in our lives, as persons and as congregations?
2. In our third century, what must we do as a denomination, so that we may continue to witness and serve as the people of the assurance?
3. What is our commitment as United Methodists, in order to proclaim the faith in our third century?

Notes

Chapter 1—A People of Assurance

1. John Wesley, *The Journal of the Rev. John Wesley, A.M.*, Standard Ed., ed. Nehemiah Curnock (London: Epworth Press, 1938), vol. 1, pp. 475-76.
2. To Samuel Walker, Vicar of Truro, in John Wesley, *The Letters of the Rev. John Wesley, A.M.*, Standard Ed., ed. John Telford (London: Epworth Press, 1931), vol. 3, p. 192.
3. Herbert B. Workman, "The Place of Methodism in the Life and Thought of the Christian Church," in *A New History of Methodism*, ed. W. G. Townsend, H. B. Workman, and G. Eayrs, vol. 1, p. 21, quoted in Wade Crawford Barclay, *Early American Methodism 1769–1844*, History of Methodist Missions (New York: Board of Missions and Church Extension of The Methodist Church, 1949), vol. 1, p. xxii.
4. Albert C. Outler, ed. *John Wesley* (New York: Oxford University Press, 1964), p. 253.
5. Emory S. Bucke, ed., *The History of American Methodism*, 3 vols. (Nashville: Abingdon Press, 1964), vol. 1, p. 74.
6. Quoted in Barclay, *Early American Methodism 1769–1844*, vol. 1, pp. 16-17.
7. Norman W. Spellmann, "The Formation of the Methodist Episcopal Church," in *History of American Methodism*, ed. Bucke, vol. 1, p. 185.
8. J. Bruce Behney and Paul H. Eller, *The History of the Evangelical United Brethren Church* (Nashville: Abingdon Press, 1979), p. 67.
9. Frederick A. Norwood, *The Story of American Methodism* (Nashville: Abingdon Press, 1974), p. 112.
10. *Ibid.*, p. 47.
11. John Wesley, *Wesley's Standard Sermons*, ed. Edward H. Sugden (London: Epworth Press, 1921), vol. 2, p. 460.

12. This is reflected in the Historical Background section of the doctrinal statements found in *The Discipline:*
"The pioneers in the traditions that flowed together in The United Methodist Church—the Wesleys, Albright, Otterbein, Boehm—understood themselves as standing in the center stream of Christian spirituality and doctrine, loyal heirs to all that was best in the Christian past. . . . Their gospel was rooted in the biblical message of God's gracious response to man's deep need, in his self-giving love revealed in Jesus Christ. Their interest in dogma as such was minimal; thus they were able to insist on the integrity of Christian truth even while allowing for a decent latitude in its interpretation. This was the point to their familiar dictum: 'As to all opinions *which do not strike at the root of Christianity,* we think and let think'" (*The Book of Discipline of The United Methodist Church, 1980* [Nashville: The United Methodist Publishing House, 1980], p. 40).
13. John Wesley, "The Character of a Methodist," in *Great Voices of the Reformation,* ed. Harry Emerson Fosdick (New York: Random House, 1952), p. 512.
14. *Ibid.,* p. 513.
15. *Book of Discipline, 1980,* p. 7.
16. Neal F. Fisher, *Context for Discovery* (Nashville: Abingdon Press, 1981), p. 120.

Chapter 2—The Fervent Spirit

1. J. Harry Haines, *Committed Locally—Living Globally* (Nashvillle: Abingdon Press, 1982), p. 12.
2. Lawrence Sherwood, "Growth and Spread, 1785–1804," in *The History of American Methodism,* ed. Emory S. Bucke (Nashville: Abingdon Press, 1964), vol. 1, pp. 364-65.
3. *Ibid.,* p. 365, partially quoted from A. H. Redford, *History of Methodism in Kentucky,* vol. 1, p. 278.
4. *Ibid.*
5. Wade Crawford Barclay, *Early American Methodism 1769–1844,* History of Methodist Missions (New York: Board of Missions and Church Extension of The Methodist Church, 1949), vol. 1, p. 123.
6. Halford E. Luccock, *Endless Line of Splendor* (Chicago: The Advance for Christ and His Church, 1950), p. 43.
7. John Wesley, *The Works of John Wesley,* 3rd ed. (London: John Mason, 1829), vol. 8, p. 269.

8. *The Book of Discipline of The United Methodist Church, 1980* (Nashville: The United Methodist Publishing House, 1980), p. 69.

9. Arthur Bruce Moss, "Methodism in Colonial America," in *History of American Methodism*, ed. Bucke, vol. 1, p. 115.

10. William R. Cannon, "Education, Publication, Benevolent Work, and Missions," in *History of American Methodism*, ed. Bucke, vol. 1, pp. 586-87.

11. Haines, *Committed Locally*, p. 27.

12. Richard M. Cameron, *Methodism and Society in Historical Perspective*, Methodism and Society (New York/Nashville: Abingdon Press, 1961), vol. 1, pp. 34-35.

13. *Ibid.*, p. 326.

14. Earl D. C. Brewer, *Continuation or Transformation?* (Nashville: Abingdon Press, 1982), p. 35.

15. *The Book of Hymns* (Nashville: The United Methodist Publishing House, 1964), No. 227.

16. Colin Williams, "Ethics, Religion and Governance" (Wye paper, 1980), quoted by Daniel Yankelovich, *New Rules: Search for Self-fulfillment in a World Turned Upside Down* (New York: Random House, 1981), p. 255.

Chapter 3—A Vital Piety

1. John Wesley, "The Character of a Methodist," in *Great Voices of the Reformation*, ed. Harry Emerson Fosdick (New York: Random House, 1952), p. 507.

2. *Ibid.*, p. 512.

3. *The Book of Discipline of The United Methodist Church, 1980* (Nashville: The United Methodist Publishing House, 1980), p. 78.

4. Neal F. Fisher, *Context for Discovery* (Nashville: Abingdon Press, 1981), p. 127.

5. *Ibid.*, p. 128.

6. *The Book of Discipline*, p. 80.

7. Fisher, *Context for Discovery*, p. 128.

8. Robert L. Wilson, *Shaping the Congregation* (Nashville: Abingdon Press, 1981), p. 50.

9. *The Book of Discipline*, p. 68.

Chapter 4—We Gather Together

1. *The Book of Discipline of The United Methodist Church, 1980* (Nashville: The United Methodist Publishing House, 1980), p. 19.

2. Matthew Simpson, ed., *Cyclopaedia of Methodism* (Philadelphia: Everts & Steward, 1872), p. 352.
3. J. Harry Haines, *Committed Locally—Living Globally* (Nashville: Abingdon Press, 1982), p. 70.
4. Robert L. Wilson, *Shaping the Congregation* (Nashville: Abingdon Press, 1981), p. 23.
5. Haines, *Committed Locally,* p. 76.
6. Wilson, *Shaping Congregation,* p. 63.

Chapter 5—To Spread Scriptural Holiness

1. Norman W. Spellman, "The Formation of the Methodist Episcopal Church," in *The History of American Methodism,* ed. Emory S. Bucke (Nashville: Abingdon Press, 1964), vol. 1, p. 226.
2. *The Book of Discipline of The United Methodist Church, 1980* (Nashville: The United Methodist Publishing House, 1980), p. 105.
3. *Ibid.,* p. 106.
4. *Ibid.,* p. 107.
5. *Ibid.,* pp. 107-8.
6. Robert K. Greenleaf, *Servant Leadership* (New York: Paulist Press, 1977), p. 52.
7. Michael Maccoby, *The Leader* (New York: Simon & Schuster, 1981), pp. 52-53.

Chapter 6—To Reform the Nation

1. Earl D. C. Brewer, *Continuation or Transformation?* (Nashville: Abingdon Press, 1982), p. 21.
2. I am indebted to Robert L. Wilson for this succinct description of the phases of racism in our society.
3. *The Book of Discipline of The United Methodist Church, 1980* (Nashville: The United Methodist Publishing House, 1980), pp. 103-4.
4. Brewer, *Continuation or Transformation?* p. 37.
5. *Ibid.,* pp. 114-15.